GO into *all the* WORLD

ONE MAN'S JOURNEY WITH GOD AND
COMPASSION INTERNATIONAL **DAVID CHALMERS**

Ark House Press
PO Box 1321, Mona Vale NSW 1660
Australia
Telephone: +61 2 9007 5376
PO Box 47212, Ponsonby, Auckland
New Zealand
Telephone: +64 9 416 8400
arkhousepress.com

All views and opinions expressed in this book are those of the author and not Compassion International.
All care has been taken to ensure the accuracy of facts and figures relating to Compassion. Please visit www.compassion.com for more information.
Please note: for the child visit accounts, names of siblings have been changed.

All Scripture references are from the New Living Translation (NLT)

Cataloguing in Publication Data:
Title: Go Into All The World
ISBN: 9780992572600 (pbk.)
Subjects: Biography
Other Authors/Contributors: Chalmers, David

Printed and bound in Australia
Design and layout by initiatemedia.net

To my dear parents, Ian and Jan:
Thank you for raising me in a God-honoring home and family.
Thank you for encouraging me to use my gifts and talents for the benefit of others.
Thank you that, although you have often struggled to understand the lifestyle of sacrificial generosity God has called me to, you never stopped supporting and providing for me.
Thank you for joining me on the Compassion journey by taking on sponsorship of two of my kids. I know you will all be blessed through the relationship.

To every person who is associated with Compassion in some way, whether you're a former sponsored child, advocate, sponsor, employee or volunteer, in the office or in the field: you are my heroes. You encourage and inspire me to continue living out my purpose, which is using what I have to help others, and ensuring that children know they are loved and valued by God. I hope this book is a blessing for you.

To Jesus, the Savior of my soul. Everything I have and everything I am is because of You. It is Your love for me and for humanity that has inspired this journey. I thank You for being with me every step of the way. I give this book to You and pray that You use it for Your glory. That is all I can ask.

David's book is a powerful combination of beholding both human pain and the hope that God brings when He steps into a life of a child. He takes us on an expedition from the favelas of Brazil to a distant island in the Philippines and to the highlands of Guatemala. You will not only experience the harsh reality of these places and what it means for a child to survive everyday hardships, but share his joy, excitement and amazement as he opens his heart as a witness on how the Church worldwide is making a difference in releasing children from those circumstances. I express my praise for this book. I had the privilege of meeting David personally and admire how he faces the unpleasant truths of our fallen world, but is moved sacrificially to react in an unselfish and biblical way. We will be moved to do something on behalf of the "least of these" after going on this amazing journey with him.

José Carlos Prem - *Country Director, Compassion International Guatemala*

This book reads like a personal journal of one man's quest to flesh out Christ's love toward children – realizing, "the kingdom of heaven belongs to such as these" (Matt.19:14b). God has given David an unquenchable desire to see the children of this world cared for holistically and saturated with the life-transforming gospel. It is truly refreshing when you encounter one whose heart is captivated by the living Christ and seeks consistently to break free of the 'affluenza' in our present culture. Though he is committed to sponsoring many children around the globe, it is my prayer as you read this book you will realize it all happens – one life at a time.

Kirby Lancaster – *Pastor, South Valley Baptist Church (Geelong, Australia)*

I have known David for several years and am honored to call him a friend. Since meeting David, I have been in awe of his passion for Compassion and seeing children across the world sponsored. I was amazed when I found out just how many children David personally sponsored, and all on a humble teacher's salary. When reading the book I was blown away to see God's grace and provision in David's life - a true testament to His word and promises. David's journey, as he travels around the world meeting the precious children he loves like his own, will leave you laughing and crying.

Sarah Hayden – *former actress/model, social worker, foster and adoptive mum*

David Chalmers takes you on a journey that evokes both anger and ecstasy. His true life experiences show us the depravity of evil and the sinister strategy of Satan. But we are not left in despair. The richness of his experiences and testimonies of the impact of Compassion's work will motivate the reader to join him in this life-changing strategy of holistic child development. Be prepared to become emotionally engaged as you read this book. It's a tribute to God's amazing grace.
Dr. Barry Slauenwhite - *President/CEO, Compassion Canada*

Change is a much loved and loudly trumpeted ideal. Conviction is the uncomfortable fuel that drives it. Compassion is the junction where the desire for change moves from the ideal to the real; where head, heart and hands connect for a cause greater than self. Read this book at your own risk; it will only make you uncomfortable, fill you with compassion and convince you to get involved to bring lasting, positive change. David Chalmers, sincerely mate, thank you.
Justin Michael Gall - *Lead Pastor, Kardinia Church, Geelong North*

Faith, love and support are a decision to me. God has decided to believe, love and support me since I was born and He uses things like the people who work for and are sponsors in Compassion to prove it. Do you want to know how my community-where before we just had violence, drugs and prostitution-has been changing step by step? With faith, love and support. How? Jesus has put churches and social projects and people such as my friend David Chalmers who cares for God's work and lives, including mine, have changed. As David says about Compassion and I am a personal proof of that - it works!
I leave you a challenge today: decide to believe, love and help a child, being and making a difference in his/her life through Compassion's ministry! "So don't get tired of doing what is good. Don't get discouraged and give up, for we will reap a harvest of blessing at the appropriate time" Galatians 6:9
Debora Silva – *former Compassion sponsored child, founding president of Compassion Alumni Brasil*

Go Into All The World is a book filled with priceless adventures that have led David to discover true joy as he obeys God and uses what God has entrusted to him. Through David's obedience, the lives of other people in different parts of the world have been changed for the better and in the process, David's own life has been transformed. God is close to the broken hearted and David encourages us all to play our part in loving people who are living in poverty to help change their lives. Go Into All The World drives home the fact that as Christ followers, loving our neighbor is not an option it is a command. The streets our neighbors live on stretch around the globe and our love must flow down these streets if we are going to make a difference on earth and news in heaven with our daily lives.

Ps Justin Gardner - *Senior Minister of Destiny Centre Christian Church (Melbourne, Australia); Author of "Crimeson" and "Small Change Big Change"*

,,

Contents

Introduction 1

Where is the Hope? 2

Who are Compassion? 3

Child Survival Program 6

Leadership Development Program 7

Visiting Homes in Compassion Communities 11

Visiting Compassion Projects 13

Pastor Letters 19

Letters from Sponsored Kids 27

How It Started for Me 32

Journey #1–Bolivia, Colombia, El Salvador 2009 33

The Crazy Compassion Plan and The Divine
Economy, 2011 43

Brazil Journey #1–September/October 2012 45

    Visiting BR-458, Projeto Sementinhas
    (Little Seeds Project) and Home Visits 49

    Visiting BR-110 Espaco Esperanca
    (Hope Space Project) and Home Visits 55

    Visiting BR-329 Centro Estudantil Vida Nova
    (New Life Student Center) and Home Visits 59

    Birthday in Brazil! 65

Brazil Journey #2–September/October 2013 71

    Birthday in Brazil 2013-A Day Like No Other 75

    The House of God in Brazil-Faith
    That Moves Mountains 83

    So Many Open Doors-Sharing Jesus With the
    Kids of Brazil 85

Journey #3–South & Central America, January 2013   89
   Visiting Allison, Danna and Olga in Mexico   91
   Visiting Josefa, Yeymi and Mayra in Guatemala   104
   Visiting Rosa and Katherine in El Salvador   115
   Visiting Jacqueline In Ecuador–A Day of
   Pure Joy and Learning About Trust   124
   Visiting Antonio in Nicaragua-The Turning Point   127
Journey #4–Philippines, April 2013   131
Journey #5–Colombia, Ecuador, Peru, September 2013   147
Journey #6–Philippines 2014   159
Someone Loves Wendy   177
Jenny and Jessica: Two Stories of Rescue,
Hope and Compassion   183
Sowing Seeds of Generosity and
Gratitude–Sharing Compassion   189
In the News–For Your Glory God   193
Innermost Thoughts From the 'Bubble of Blessing'   195
A Tribute to True Heroes   199
Stories from the Compassion Projects and Beyond   201
The Great Visit Debate   207
The Good Word (Bible Verses)   211
Why I Visit My Sponsored Kids and
Sponsor with Compassion   215
A Final Challenge   219
Websites   221
About The Author   222

Introduction

My purpose for writing this book is simple. I want to paint some pictures for you.

I want to tell you about Compassion International, what they do and how they are fighting poverty and transforming lives motivated by faith, integrity and God's love.

I want to open your eyes and give you just a glimpse of what life is like for people in the developing world, as well as the challenges and circumstances they face.

I want to show, viewed through the lens of my personal experience, what a difference one person can make in the lives of others when you trust God as your provider, discard a life of self, comfort and ease, and decide to give generously and sacrificially.

I want to let my light shine, but for God's glory (Matthew 5:16). My involvement with Compassion has cost me a whole lot but ultimately it is all for God and because of God. There are stories in here that simply need to be told, in order to set an example for others and motivate them to help.

Contained in the pages of this book are stories of heartbreak, despair, tragedy, hopelessness and sadness, and yet you will also encounter joy, faith, love, contentment, generosity and hope for the future. I can assure you that you will in some way be impacted, challenged and transformed and I hope that you are moved to positive action in response to what you read.

Where is the Hope?

Ana Cristina is a beautiful 14-year-old girl who lives in the city of Fortaleza, Brazil. Over the last three years her family has been ravaged by drugs, murder and revenge, and they have been forced into hiding. I visited her home and community in October 2013 and even though I knew about her family situation, seeing the reality of it with my own eyes shocked me to the core.

When I arrived at the house I was greeted shyly and cautiously by Cristina's parents. I really wanted to know more about what the family had been through so I asked Mama, but she understandably didn't want to dwell on their situation too much, having lost one brother to murder and the other one in jail. As we talked, they gradually started opening up. This is what I found out.

Outside Cristina's house runs a stream of sewage. She is one of eleven people living in a one-bedroom house. The fence surrounding the property is topped up with broken bottle edges and barbed wire. Neither of her parents are able to work because there are simply no jobs available in the community. They live off a small allowance from the government which is the equivalent of about $25 a week. The house they are living in belongs to her grandmother and when she dies they will be at the mercy of other extended family members. The community is incredibly dangerous: they cannot leave the house after 7pm and can't leave the kids at home alone any time. Only three houses in the street are actually occupied because of the danger. There is marshland out the back which floods when it rains. Cristina's mother was 13 when she had the first of her six children and her oldest son recently had a baby with a 14-year-old girl.

As I was listening to this story, it just kept getting worse and worse. For the first time in my life I came face-to-face with true hopelessness and it was horrifying. The question that screamed at the front of my mind over and over was "*Where is the hope for these people*?"

That HOPE is what this book is about.

Who are Compassion?

Thankfully, Ana Cristina and her family have hope because of a wonderful organization called Compassion International. I started sponsoring Cristina through Compassion at the start of 2011 and, as a result, made the decision to enter her world.

In 1952 Rev. Everett Swanson, an American Pastor, was on a successful preaching tour in South Korea during the Korean War when he encountered the bitter poverty of Korea's unwanted children. Upon his return to the United States, Rev. Swanson established a program that allowed caring people to provide food, shelter, education, medical care and Christian training for Korean orphans. 62 years later Compassion International works in 26 countries and cares for over 1.4 million babies, children and students.[1]

Compassion works through local churches to provide child development programs to deliver children who are from economic, physical, social and spiritual poverty, enabling them to become responsible, fulfilled Christian adults. They link each child with one sponsor who has the privilege of providing for many of that child's material needs, as well as forming a relationship with them through regular letters. Words of life and encouragement are just as, if not more important than, the financial support. People need to know that they are loved, valued and special, and one of the worst things about poverty is that it steals a person's sense of hope, worth and value.

Children who are registered and sponsored with Compassion meet at a place called a Project or Student Center. This is often the only safe place they have in their world. The workers who care for them are almost all volunteers from the partner church, giving up their time and literally giving their lives simply to show these children love. Here they receive often their only nutritious meal for the day, medical care, education

---

1 http://www.compassion.com

support, social skills and an opportunity to have an eternal relationship with the Creator of the universe. No one is forced to convert or believe anything, but when a person comes face-to-face with the relentless, extravagant, sacrificial love of God through all Compassion does, it can be hard to resist.

Compassion operates by the four Cs:
    Child-focused
    Christ-centered
    Church-based
    Committed to integrity

Jesus is at the center of all Compassion does. I love this from Mark Hanlon, a senior vice-president at Compassion:

> *"The marketing consultants sat across the table from the Compassion clients they were about to pitch. While nobody actually documented the exact words the consultants uttered, their recommendation and the seismic crater it created are now part of Compassion International's cultural lore.*

> *"If you really want to grow your share of the market," the consultant recommended, "the best thing you could do is drop the name of Jesus from your tagline. There are plenty of people who would love to support what you do to assist children. But they can't relate to the 'Jesus thing.'"*

> *Releasing children from poverty in Jesus's name was more than the tagline designed into Compassion's corporate mark. It was our mission and methodology all wrapped in one. Did Compassion want to grow? Absolutely. We believed in our cause and its effectiveness. But did we think that diluting our distinctiveness -- what gave us our strength and identity -- was worth the assumed growth? Not at all. The pitch was essentially over.*

I suppose the assumption by the consultant was that Jesus simply couldn't compete. Instead of drawing minds and hearts into the cause, his name would push people away."[2]

This commitment to integrity is just one reason why I have been such a passionate and committed Compassion sponsor over the last seven years. Compassion is God's business, and that is something I will shout from the rooftops all my life. Just in case you need more proof, here's an interesting fact:

In 2002, 27,000 children were sponsored through Compassion Australia. Keeping in mind that the following ten years were like an economic rollercoaster *and* Compassion relies completely on sponsors for its revenue, in 2012 the number of sponsored children reached 100,000. That's an increase of over 300%.

After visiting Cristina, I asked the Compassion workers if their situation was extreme or typical. Unfortunately it's the same story for many children and families in that community. Honestly, the only spark of Hope in Cristina's life comes from the existence of Compassion and the church, bringing God's love through providing for their basic needs and giving them an opportunity for a future, both in this life and the next.

2   http://www.huffingtonpost.com/mark-hanlon/that-jesus-thing_b_4816733.html

Child Survival Program

Traditional child development programs have focused on supporting school-aged children. At some point, the good people at Compassion became aware of the need to address the issue of child mortality and the importance of good health in the first five years of life in developing countries. Thus the Child Survival Program (CSP) was born.

The CSP provides pregnant women and their babies up to 3 years of age with, among other things, health care, nutrition and hygiene. It is mainly home-based, where a staff member visits and assists the woman in her home. The mother is also taught income-generating skills to help her lift herself and her family out of poverty and give her children an opportunity at making a future for themselves.

The CSP provides the 'stepping-stone' to the CDSP (sponsorship program), although a child doesn't have to be in the CSP before they can be registered for sponsorship. Compassion knows that if the child has spent the first three years of their life being cared for in the CSP, they will be healthy and ready to enter the CDSP.[3]

When I was in the Philippines, the team I traveled with saw the CSP in action. We were divided into three groups to enable us to interact with the mothers of the CSP and their babies. We saw them take part in a cooking class and make bags from cereal boxes, which they are able to sell to earn some money for themselves to provide for their family. Normally they use a sewing machine to put the bags together, but at the time the machine was broken so they were sewing by hand.

It was our team's joy and privilege to buy several bags from the mothers to take home with us, and hopefully they were able to replace the sewing machine.

---

3   http://www.compassion.com/help-babies.htm

Leadership Development Program

Because Compassion's goal is to raise up Christian leaders in their communities and countries, it didn't made sense that kids were shown the door as soon as they finished school. That's where the Leadership Development Program (LDP) comes in. The LDP involves identifying Compassion-assisted youth who have leadership potential and assists them with college tuition, textbooks and other school-related expenses. They are also set up with a sponsor who becomes like a mentor to them. The cost and commitment required from sponsors is on a whole different level to child sponsorship, but it is equally as important.[4]

I've been privileged to meet quite a few LDP students and graduates in the last few years, and every time I do it makes my heart jump for joy because they are the success stories. Whatever they end up doing, if they do it well and to the glory of God, they are the proof that Compassion sponsorship is effective and it works. I want to share the stories of four of them.

Richmond Wandera grew up in extreme poverty in the Naguru slum near Kampala, Uganda. As a child, he battled malaria more than ten times and understood from an early age that life was fragile. But when Richmond's father was murdered, he lost all hope of a life worth living. It wasn't until he was brought into a local Compassion child development center, when he started receiving healthcare, education, love, and best of all, a knowledge of God that he started to see life differently.

Richmond excelled in school, and after graduating, he was chosen to enter Compassion's *Leadership Development Program*, which provided him the opportunity to earn a university degree. Upon completing college, Richmond was overwhelmed with a burning desire to see the spiritual state of his country change. He was accepted to attend

---

4   http://www.compassion.com/student-leader.htm

the Moody Graduate School and Theological Seminary in Chicago to complete his Master's Degree.

A year after he began his studies at Moody, Richmond conceived the idea of free monthly theological training for pastors in Uganda, along with provision of study resources and mentorship programs. From this, he founded the Pastors' Discipleship Network (PDN). The ministry of PDN has spread rapidly through enthusiastic partners to more than 4000 pastors in Uganda, Kenya, South Sudan and Democratic Republic of Congo.[5]

Michelle Tolentino was born and raised in the Philippines. In her words *"I was surrounded by drug users, prostitutes, and gamblers. During that time, my father was also a drug abuser and he ended up leaving us for some time. It all was a picture of hopelessness, a picture that communicated that our father didn't really care for us or love us. The people around me would always tell me: "Michelle, you are so ugly just like your father and you'll grow up like him." Those are the words that were spoken into my heart and those were cruel words of anger and hatred. So, therefore I didn't have a future, because no one would love me. So, I felt so hopeless, that I really didn't matter and that I was not important."[6]*

Michelle's aunt, who was the only Christian person she knew, took her to a local church and registered in the Compassion Project there. Michelle was sponsored at age six and her life changed forever. Her sponsors spoke words of life into her, such as *"'Michelle, you are so beautiful. We love you. We are praying for you. We are so proud of you."*

"Compassion hasn't just released me from poverty, but it has gotten me to dream big, to make a difference and never ever to forget my country, even if my country is living in poverty. They taught me to always give back, to always make a difference for the cause of Christ. A lot of people, when they are poor, try to become rich. But Compassion taught me is that it is not

---

5   http://www.compassion.com.au/news_item.php?intid=1525
6   http://www.positive-entertainment.com/interviews/michelletolentino

about me. It's about other people and God. Always, sow seeds and plant seeds in the lives of other people, which we can reap in the future."[7]

Michelle founded an organization called *Made in Hope* where, with God's help, she is 'Restoring Hope and Crafting a Future for Exploited Women and Children.'

I met **Debora Silva** when I travelled to Brazil in 2013. She is a former sponsored child and LDP graduate. She is now the President of the Compassion Alumni of Brazil.

The Compassion Alumni has been set up to connect and support people who have graduated from the Child Sponsorship Program and are doing or have graduated from the Leadership Development Program. The LDP had their first group of graduating students only recently, so the Alumni is in its early stages. Debora said there is still some confusion about why the Alumni actually exists and what its purpose is. As the president, she is a pioneer and it's her job to make this clear to people.

When I was in Brazil I was privileged to attend a meeting to hear about a strategy Debora and her team have devised in order to raise funds for the Alumni. It is called '*Speak, Hable, Fale!*' and involves teaching people Spanish and English for a fraction of the price of the language schools that exist. This is to provide people with a skill that can help them earn an income and help their families escape poverty.

When Debora was three months old, she was very sick and was given about three days to live. Her parents were new Christians and prayed over her along with other family members, some of whom were involved in the occult. However, they all wanted the same thing: Debora to live. Her mother prayed: "*God, if you have a purpose for Debora in this earth, and I believe on this, I just believe you will make it since taking all the disease from her body now.*" And He did.[8]

---

7   http://blog.compassion.com/michelle-tolentino
8   http://forshamim.blogspot.com/2013/08/deboras-story.html

God has remained faithful to Debora. He has not removed the challenges from her life, but has helped her overcome them. After Debora graduated from the Child Sponsorship Program she was accepted in the first group of LDP students in Brazil–one of 20 from a graduating class of 400.

She is a leader, a visionary and a role model for other Compassion sponsored children, and she is aware of this. She has found that God-given purpose her mother knew she had at three months old.

When in the Philippines in 2013, our team met a group of amazing LDP students. I talked with a wonderful little 17-year-old called **Angie**. She is the youngest of four kids and was the only one sponsored in her family. At the time she was studying accounting and leading a Bible study group for ten girls aged 13-15 years old. She is truly a shining light and an example for these girls to look up to. Her Dad died when she was three and her mum is actually a Compassion Project worker. Her sister has a baby and hopes to be registered in the Child Survival Program. God is so clearly moving in Angie's life and it was such a privilege to able to pray with and for her at the end of the night.

Visiting Homes in Compassion Communities

In the developed world, it is fairly easy to hide reality. You can tidy up a bit, put the kettle on, engage in meaningless small talk and pretend to your guests everything is okay.

When you visit a home in the developing world, what you see is what you get. What is before you is reality. There is no hiding or pretending everything is okay when it clearly isn't, and more than once it has floored me.

There are many people who sponsor children but are hesitant to go any further with it other than putting the picture on the fridge and paying the money. They often can't tell people where their child is from, how old they are or even their name. No effort is made to write regular letters or do some research to find out about their community.

I can understand this deliberate ignorance or disconnection to a point. If I keep them at arm's length, my heart can't get hurt by what I might find out about their reality. It is a risk for those of us who are secure, comfortable and materially wealthy.

For me, the day I truly broke free from this ignorance and disconnection as a sponsor came a couple of years ago. I was already a passionate Compassion sponsor and I was singing the song 'Hosanna' in church, when the reality of the lyrics hit me. Since I have been in church basically my whole life, I have a habit of singing words without really thinking about them much. When you're singing about God and to God, this habit is best avoided.

On this day, the words that stuck out to me were: "*Show me how to love like you have loved me....Break my heart for what breaks yours, everything I am for your Kingdom's cause....*" I prayed "*God, I want you to make those words a reality in my life, no matter what the cost.*"

Well, I can tell you that God honored that request and there have been many times since that day that I wish I kept my big mouth shut. After I said that prayer asking God to break my heart, I knew it was a risk worth taking. Growing up in Australia, my own upbringing was idyllic and somewhat sheltered, being in churches and Christian schools the whole time (though I wouldn't change it for anything). I was always safe, comfortable and I had everything I could ever want or need. God knew it was going to take something massive to change my perspective. He has certainly given me but a glimpse of what breaks His heart and this has come through the Compassion home visits.

Visiting Compassion Projects

One of Compassion's fundamental strategies is partnering with local churches because underpinning everything they do is the belief that a relationship with Jesus is the ultimate release from poverty, in this life and in eternity. The church is the vehicle that God uses to bring His Kingdom to earth, so it makes sense to partner with them.

Everything else that Compassion offers flows from this love of, and for, God: the food, clean water, medical care, educational assistance, income-generating skills and pairing with a loving sponsor, often from the other side of the world.

Compassion cares for the child holistically: this includes physically, economically, spiritually and socio-emotionally. Although they are best known for the school-age Child Sponsorship Program, there are actually three main programs:
- **Child Survival Program**, which takes care of pregnant women, caregivers and babies up to three years old
- **Child Development Sponsorship Program**, which is the school-aged sponsorship program for children from 3 to 22 years old, depending on the country.
- **Leadership Development Program**, which provides sponsorship and mentoring for students wanting to go to College. It is a very rigorous process aimed at building up Christian leaders who want to serve their community and their country.[9]

I can assure you that Compassion does not come heroically thundering into a village saying *"Never fear! Compassion is here!"* They make sure the community knows it is the Church that is doing all the hard work and sacrifice, and their motivation is not personal recognition or kudos, but to share the love of God with the children and families in the community.

---

9   http://www.compassion.com

Partnering with Compassion is not an easy process, and to ensure integrity and accountability there are quality standards the church must meet in terms of their ability to care for the children and families. They must have a certain number of members and particular facilities before they can be considered for partnership.

One thing the church must have is a space for the children to meet during the week in order for Compassion's programs to be carried out. This space is often called a Project or a Student Center. Depending on the Center, children may attend anywhere from once a week to every day, but they must live within 30 minutes travel distance in order to get the most out of Compassion's programs.

Compassion Projects are seriously my favorite places in the world. It is quite difficult to describe to someone who has not experienced it for themselves, but in all my visits I could literally feel the difference between the atmosphere outside the gates and inside the Project.

Because Compassion intentionally serves the poorest of the poor, the communities are often hopeless and desperate places. I have felt the danger and the darkness that is a by-product of this messed-up world, poverty and the evil that comes with it.

Once inside the gates, without fail, it is a completely different universe. The Love of God is there, pure and simple. Human compassion is nice but it just doesn't measure up. The children have a safe place where they can be loved unconditionally, encouraged, fed, cleaned, and are just free to be kids. It is incredible to witness. The food and drink they receive is often their only decent meal for the day and their only access to clean drinking water. Some of my sponsored kids did not have access to water in their homes, so thank God for Compassion.

The environment of the Project is always very colorful and child-friendly. Art work and decorations are on the walls. The children are celebrated and acknowledged. There are educational posters and children's work on display everywhere. Definitely a safe and loving place to be.

At the Project the children receive help with their school work. They are taught practical things like hygiene and taking care of their bodies. They are taught to recognize abuse and how to say "*no*." They are taught about making wise choices in relating to other people that will keep them out of trouble.

As they grow older, the children are taught income-generating skills like baking, computers, cosmetology (hair and makeup), how to make bags or necklaces. One of the aims of Compassion is to teach the children and families how to look after themselves and get them out of there, because as soon as a family can sufficiently provide for their own needs they are well on the way to being released from poverty.

The children are recognized and celebrated as unique and special individuals who have been created by God for a purpose. This flies in the face of everything they have been taught in their lives to this point in their homes and communities. Poverty tells them they are nothing: worthless, useless, hopeless and things will never change or get better. This lie has robbed millions of their God-given destiny. Compassion and the church are fighting against this.

At the Project, Compassion's motivation is never hidden or made secret. They are there to share the love of God with the children and families. No-one is forced to convert, believe or go to church. However, when such unearned and undeserved Love is shown with no strings attached, people are bound to get curious. There have been many churches who have started small but through their involvement with Compassion they have grown and seen their communities change for the better.

I particularly love the story of a certain Compassion Project in a gang-infested community in Brazil. One day the bars from the church windows were stolen and the Pastor complained to the local drug lord. The next day the bars were returned and the church never had any theft problems again. Even the dangerous criminals respect Compassion because they know Compassion are providing a future for their children that they themselves cannot through their lives of lawlessness.

The majority of Compassion Project workers are volunteers from the partner church. They are generally skilled in the area they work, whether they are teaching the children, in the kitchen, cleaning the facilities or dealing with the finances. Many of them are poor themselves but believe enough in Compassion's ministry that they sacrifice a better job or opportunity somewhere else in order to serve God by caring for the children and families. This never ceases to amaze and inspire me, and I always make a point of encouraging and praying for the Project workers when I visit a Project.

Another testament to the impact of the Compassion Projects is the number I've been to where I've met young people who have graduated from the Child Sponsorship Program but have returned to their Project in order to help or teach. They clearly recognize what a gift of God these places are and rather than moving on with their lives and consigning their time at the Project to their distant past, they choose to come back and provide living examples of the effectiveness of Compassion and the grace of God to the children at the Project. What they are saying through their presence is *"You might be poor now, but there is Hope. Look at me, I was once in your position, but through Compassion God has released me and given me a purpose. He can do the same for you."*

If you were to visit a Compassion Project, this is what you will experience:
* **Kids**. There might be many or there might be a few, depending on if it's an activity day. Either way they will be joyous, they will be curious, they will be animated and they will LOVE that you are there. Even better if you love to sing and play games and you don't let the language barrier get in the way of having a great time.

* You will be taken on a **tour of the Project**. There are no hidden or secret places at a Compassion Project. Their transparency and willingness to answer any questions honestly and openly continually amazes me.

* You will see **cabinets stacked with child records**. Every single little detail about every child is meticulously recorded: medical, educational, home situation, letters and gifts from sponsors, hopes and dreams for the future. Every dollar spent is audited at three levels. Massive integrity.

* You will receive **words of profound gratitude and thankfulness** that just might make you cry. Until we have been to a Compassion Project and actually talked to the children and Project workers, we have no idea what our relatively insignificant dollar amount and letters that we might send out of a sense of duty mean to those on the receiving end. For so many families the care of Compassion and the church is literally the difference between life and death.

* You will get a '**dinner and a show**' (will probably be lunch). Compassion Projects get incredibly excited when they know visitors are coming and put so much effort into making them feel welcome. It is always so humbling to receive the generosity and love of the poor. They will put on a feast of delicious food for you and feed you until you *"can't stands no more."*

* You may be invited, or 'encouraged,' to get up and **perform something** yourself (so be prepared). Fortunately I am no shrinking violet in front of a crowd, so I happily grabbed any opportunity I got to sing, play badly-out-of-tune guitars, get on the drums, teach crazy action-songs or teach them a bit about Australia.

I have had songs, dances, banners, balloons, PowerPoint slideshows and even incredibly talented bands of teenagers play in my honor, all because I made the simple decision to go and visit.
I have been given little handmade cards and gifts made with pure love by kids I didn't even know.
I have had children pray for me and ask to lay their hand on my head as they did so.
I have had children learn a few words of English just so they could greet me in person with a little speech.

The act of sponsoring a child and visiting a Compassion Project.
The love and hospitality of the people at the Compassion Project.

These are both responses to the extravagant and lavish Love of God. Unearned and undeserved but given anyway, with nothing expected in return in terms of our ability to repay that love.

Compassion Projects=Love, Joy, Faith, Hope, Sacrifice, Generosity, Hospitality, Safety, Music, Dancing, Playing, *Kids Free To Be Kids!*

Pastor Letters

The Pastors of Compassion partner churches are among my heroes and I've been privileged to meet many. They are sacrificially giving and sharing God's love in desperately poor places and investing in the lives of children and families.

One fantastic initiative Compassion has developed are the Pastor Letters. Each Pastor of a Compassion partner church writes a yearly letter to the sponsors. Far from being manufactured 'sponsor-inducing propaganda,' the letters give a fascinating and necessary insight into details of the reality and the challenges the community is facing, as well as the impact Compassion is having on the children, families and the community. Over the last seven years I have sponsored 54 children from 26 countries and I've received my fair share of Pastor letters. I wanted to share with you a glimpse of Compassion's impact through the eyes of Church partner Pastors:

Partnering with Compassion International has enabled us to open the gospel's door not to just to the children but to their parents as well for them to grow in the Lord as much as their children. We have been assisting our children to live a healthy life as well as to know how to prevent diseases or some physical problems. Most important we give them a chance to try to take on the world for Jesus!

Many of our parents have come to us in deep confidence to share that they have seen how the lives of their children have changed drastically especially in the way they relate to their parents, showing more respect for them and for all the people that they get in touch with.

Dear sponsor, your words included in letters for our children are priceless! It draws a smile from ear to ear on each child every time they read their letters, because they know they are loved by someone far away! Your role in the lives of our children is extremely important, and we are so grateful for having you in our lives!

May God bless you abundantly, and I want to dearly thank you for your generosity shown through your support for Yeymi. You and I are drawing this community closer to God, and your support is such a blessing for each of our children!

Thank you for giving us an opportunity to improve the life of children as well as families. Every moment the children are enjoying is because of Compassion and sponsors like you.

Now children are coming to the Center. Children are being developed educationally, physically, spiritually and socially. Now the children are free from malnutrition and are healthy and active. And they are excelling in the education, and I am happy the Center had vacation program where children heard many stories of faithful servants, new songs and memory verses, and the lessons were taught through puppet show. I am sure the children will grow in faith and become good citizens with values of our country.

At this moment we see ourselves as the shepherd who walks ahead and takes care of the flock of sheep, the children. To us the sheep seem so pure and innocent. Proud of the sheep, we see them as a beautiful group. As the pastors we care and pray for the sheep and we bring them to the faithful pastor, the Son of God, Jesus Christ. We enjoy participating in this mission as shepherds of the sheep.

Jesus has allowed us as a church in this area to achieve our dreams, goals, vision. We are certain our Lord Himself has approved the mission, first because we believe that it is in His heart. He has given us desire to reach our children and youth for him in order that they could find the truth that sets us free from captivity, poverty, misery and ignorance.

We can tell you that the letters we have received from sponsors have been delivered to the children, and when they receive them we see their smiles. Their hearts fill with joy especially when they see pictures or other things from their sponsor family. They now understand that there is someone who loves them and now they are part of their families.

Our vision in the future for our children is to see them ready in all the areas of their lives. We dream to have at our Center the best conditions spiritually, personnel and facilities to continue fulfilling our commitment. We know that united with sponsors like you we can continue creating opportunities for our children, that is so hurt by many causes that mix to destroy them. But with the help of God, we will win the victory in their lives.

The letters from sponsors always produce happiness when they come to our children in the Center. They keep each letter with joy. Some of them have told me about sponsors' emotive letters with content of love and appreciation for them. The children and the staff and I all thank God for the sponsors and pray for you.

Our sponsors' help has indeed had a great impact on our children and their families. They value the program and many of them have been released from poverty. They have learned skills that enable them to support themselves and their families.

Now almost 60 percent of our children attend church, Sunday school and youth ministries. We are also working with the children's parents. We have established a plan called "Felipe Plan" and it is about winning and involving more people for Christ. Now there are committed people to visit the parents and put them in the Lord's path. This plan is blessed with our prayers.

As pastor and God's servant, I feel so privileged to serve. It is our vision to work with our youth. We pray that they will get salvation and become great leaders and citizens. The mission of the church is that these children and teenagers believe in God as their Savior and that they are developing strong values. It is a joy to see our children smile every time they receive letters, pictures and cards from their sponsors.

I feel privileged that the church supports these children through the support of the Compassion partnership. The church is the main spiritual provider to the children, their families and the community at large.

Here at the Center, children are taught income-generating skills which they can't receive anywhere else. They also receive medical treatment whenever necessary.

My vision is to serve these children diligently and bring them to God so that they may become responsible men and women of great importance. They are the future leaders of our church and our nation at large.

The relationship between sponsors and children has been of great importance and value to them. The lovely letters and photos mean so much to them and will always be a remembrance of you. The children feel more loved and valued when they receive letters, and they keep praying that God will bless you abundantly.

We thank God that He extends our ministry in the community to help these unprivileged children. Our church has opportunities to fill what's lacking in their lives. We are like their fathers and mothers, ready to give them and their families guidance, and offering them the salvation of Christ.

We would like to thank God that we have you as the faithful sponsor for Teeraphat. We realize that you are a vital part in this ministry. Your financial giving enables us to minister to the unprivileged children, who are precious. It allows the children, their families and others in the community to know and be touched by the love of God through action. May God bless you so much for your prayers.

I would like to share with you and let you know the way your help has been a blessing to children and youth as well as the church of God. Through your sponsorship, our children and youth have been escaped from bad companies - for example, gangs, drug abuse, robbery, prostitution, etc.

It is my feeling and hope as pastor of the church that your sponsorship carried on through Compassion International will continue to help the churches for the child and youth sponsorship, because the church is the Center for the spiritual, educational, physical and social affairs. This service to children and youth has brought big changes through your help since we started this partnership with Compassion International Tanzania.

Our program is impacting children's lives. The children are always glad to come to the Center here at our church because they often face difficulties at their homes and in their area. When they are at Center we provide them with games and a place where they can play together and enjoy different types of activities.

At the Child Development Center the children learn many things about health, hygiene practices, and good manners. The Center workers and teachers love the children and know each of them by name. They teach them classes to enrich their skills, such as painting, sewing, and music. But above all, we take time to teach them about Jesus Christ. We pray for each child and conduct regular Bible classes. Each year we have many children that make professions of faith in Jesus, and as a result, several family members have started attending our Sunday church services.

We all admit that Compassion's Child Sponsorship Program is a gift from God to Haiti, especially to the underprivileged children. We thank all of our sponsors, everywhere they are, for making such a great impact in the community of Sanoix.

I feel happy with the group of helpers and tutors, men and women of God who have wanted to serve with the heart to these little ones. They love them deeply and know their names, their tastes, their strengths, their houses, their parents, their dreams and hopes. We focus deeply on them and teach them about health and hygiene, good conduct and relations with others.

The wish of my heart is to serve my city in the name of my Lord Jesus, and I am grateful for this privilege that I am given to see my boys and girls and teenagers happy and with high self-esteem and see that they are being changed radically.

I want you to know that your sponsor support means a lot to Paola. I admire you and I know that God will continue to bless you. Our children need the most to feel loved, and sponsors show them that abundantly. When they receive the letters and the photos they are really happy and that makes them feel special. Many of these kids cry next to me when they read the letters.

I also want to tell you that the same way you assist our Luz de Esperanza Student Center, we also receive the support of many sponsors for our children through Compassion, which are transformed into wonderful blessings for all the children in this Child Development Center.

All the sponsored children live in the poorest region of our community, and the protection that they receive from Compassion and our church at the Center is practically the only sign of life and hope they have. Our program is a place for the children not only to grow integrally but is a blessing place as it is an oasis in the desert, and you the sponsors make it possible with your generous sponsorships.

I must share with you that your help reaches more than the sponsored children. Our Center and Compassion have a partnership to reach the parents of sponsored children in family orientation meetings, vocational workshops and courses to help them improve their lives and income generation. In this regard we are intentional in presenting the gospel so they can know that God is the real fountain of life.

It is important for me to indicate here that we and our community have never benefited from any support or care of the kind Compassion is giving us. We are not taking this for granted, and I personally believe that the ministry of Compassion is God's blessing for all the children of our community and even our country.

The good news today is that we are so thankful to God for the Compassion ministry because our program is making a very big and meaningful impact in the lives of our children, their parents and the community as a whole. Health, education, socio-emotional and spiritual needs of all 200 children of our Center are fully being taken care of. At the moment only 89 children of our Center have sponsors, and we are praying that God will grant each of the 111 remaining children the grace to have a sponsor as well.

The participation of our children in our program has given the opportunity to many parents to join our church, and we thank God for their lives. My aim is to continue serving our community through the Compassion ministry and to see our little children grow and become true, fulfilled adult Christians, capable to carry out the Great Commission of our Lord Jesus Christ.

Our sponsored children are very excited. The support they receive at the Center has given them some freedom from their poverty, from anxiety related to their parents' unemployment, and from sickness and rejection.

The staff members' work is fruitful and souls are getting saved. My vision is to bring the population to repentance; at every meeting, parents and authorities fill the temple and show their approval for the Center's activities.

Receiving pictures, letters and gifts from sponsors contributes to a sense of happiness and fulfilment.

The work is hard, but the results are so precious to us that they motivate us to go on. I therefore ask you to pray for them, for our entire Center, and for our holistic training program, which aims to make Jesus known. Peace, life and happiness are found in Him.

For that reason we want to thank you for the children of our Child Development Center, their parents and of course me, because of your support of this great program. As a pastor I have been able to see during these years the way the children have improved in every area of their lives and they are becoming in good citizens. We do not get tired of thanking God for putting sponsors in these children's path and for contributing to their formation.

My desire is to keep encouraging you to help us in this beautiful task where we form people to contribute to a better future for those who are just growing in our society. May God bless you from the highness and multiply you a hundred percent for your contribution; these children need you for living, and I wish these children grow healthy and strong, and we want that the Center's influence is reflected in their behavior.

Before I close this letter, I would like to say something special to you who have been touched by God. Only the eternity will reveal how valuable your decision is. The prayers from the needy ones go up to heaven as in a bunch, but the answer from God comes down like an arrow in direction of the one He loves - His chosen one. In our case, I believe that in God's answer the arrows turn into two: one comes down upon the sponsored child and the other upon the sponsor. Rest assured that every day our children pray for you.

This is what you've showed with the daily support, financial and spiritual. You are the children's happiness, because for the children you are the fathers that some of them didn't have, and the mothers that give them love and affection. We trust in the Lord that He will provide you to continue supporting such a beautiful cause for the wellbeing of the children, who are the kingdom of heaven. The Lord will do great things on them to transform lives and the world.

I want you to know how much I appreciate your support as a sponsor of this child. The children feel loved and valued. We share with them the names of their sponsors, and whenever they receive a letter or photo, they feel very happy. This makes them feel special. For them, it is important to know that there are people who care and pray for them. We are grateful with all our hearts for the love that you have shown.

Letters from Sponsored Kids

In 2009 I took my first trip with Compassion, visiting my kids in Bolivia, Colombia and El Salvador. At that time I was a maybe-twice-a-year letter writer because I just had no idea how important they were. I received my wake-up call when I could sense the disappointment from one of my kids about how little I'd written. I was awakened to the reality that, while they appreciate the financial support, for many of the kids their sponsor is the closest they have to a friend or even a parent. If they don't hear from us they start to question things and maybe even doubt the love of God, as tragic as that is.

It still took a couple of years, but eventually I ramped it up and since 2010 I have written monthly to my many sponsored kids, and I always send photos. Compassion has made it clear that sponsorship is about relationship and they've made it *so easy* to write letters (you can even do it online).

When I made the decision to write monthly our relationships were blessed out of sight. The children really opened up and I have received incredibly honest letters about fighting parents, deaths, job losses, fears and worries, as well as triumphs, salvations, baptisms, hopes and dreams. **Sponsors, please know your letters are treasured, re-read many times and always kept in a special place**. I have sat in classrooms and watched children gaze lovingly at a letter they had received and hold it close, almost as if they were actually embracing their sponsor.

Although the system is not perfect and sponsors sometimes have to wait longer than they would like to between letters, I do take my hat off to the Project workers, volunteers and translators, without whom we wouldn't hear from the kids at all. I realize that with the diverse number of countries and communities Compassion works in, communication on such a mass scale is ridiculously hard, so we should continue to ask for patience and forgiveness each time we look at an empty letterbox and give another grumble.

When I was in the Philippines, I was very happy to witness letter writing in action. Apparently there are some insufferable cynics who think some guy sits in an office and writes out imaginary letters by imaginary sponsor children. I can't fathom that level of cynicism, but I've heard that some people have that view. Anything to get out of giving to the poor I guess. To those people let me say: *Sponsored children do exist, and they sure as heck write you letters!!*

Here is a sample of some of the letters my kids have written me. Humbling indeed.

I have the honor of having a sponsor like you; you are one of my best examples to follow because it is wonderful to read the letters you sent to me. It is as if I were close to you; I am happy, like with your presence in my humble home. It was so great when you were with me. I will never forget that day. If I lived with you it would be a great life, sad-happy, full of blessings and joy. When I write letters to you I get inspired because I imagine you with me. I don't know how, but it is like magic writing these words because I do not say them, my heart says them, and with lots of love.

In my free time I read a book or the Bible because sometimes I get scared. It's like living as you read it. I like to read inspirational thoughts and I like visiting home. I wrote something: "Dreams come true asking God for wisdom because to Him, nothing is impossible; we have to open our heart and ask with faith." This pushes me to go on when I am in trouble my family or in my life.

I pray for you every day because now I know that dreams can come true asking God with all the heart. Thank you for all the time you gave me and for giving me your love and attention (*written after I visited her*)

Do you know something incredible? You are a hero for Jacque, she would like to be like you when she grows up – a great professional. She wants to work with children, and the same as you, to be mature spiritually in faith. Jacque wants that you never get apart from Jesus. Jacque would like to be like you because you follow Jesus Christ's footprints. Jacque asks God that you come to Ecuador. She wants to see your eyes and tell you she loves you.

When I get older, my dream is to become a teacher like you. I want to help my family and my younger siblings. There is nothing in my life that I am worried about because I always believe that God will provide everything for me and will shower His blessings to my family.

I hope that you will find someone who will take good care of you and love you so much. I know God will send her to you, because a good man like you deserves to be happy.

Someday I would like to sponsor children like you do.

I feel very excited to write you again, and tell you that I'm proud that you be my sponsor. I loved your letters and your pictures. It's amazing what you do for us, and I say "we" because all the children who appear in the picture are your children. Sponsor, my classmates were amazed to watch every one of those children. Thanks. I don't know how to pay you for all what you do for us.

You are so special to me, you are a valuable person and your letters make me happy. I always remember when you came to visit me, I will never forget those moments we shared, I enjoyed when we were with all my family. I thank God for having a great sponsor, you are a nice friend and I pray for you. I thank you so much for all your help and your love.

I always pray for God to heal your knee completely. God is powerful and he sent a prophet to prophesy about dried bones and a strong wind came and he prophesied and the bones had life and they got up; God is a supernatural God. Do you believe it? God is the one who strengths us. Do you believe God can heal you? If you do, I will send that word in the Jesus of Nazareth's name.

I also thank you for the Biblical verses you sent me, they teach me more about God and it strengthen me in my spiritual life and wisdom.

When I read your letter, my self-esteem was strengthened, and I was able to see life in a different way. Thank you so much for giving me advice. It's very important to me.

You are great and I love you very much, the words that you write me are a blessing for my life and strengthen my spirit and esteem.

I love you very much, and I'm very proud of you because you help many children like me and you make them smile each day. May God guide your path forever!

Please give your nieces and nephews lots of hugs, especially Amelia, and when you do, think of me.

Please, when you come here, please bring me the baby Amelia, because I just saw her through the picture and I like her very much

I want to dedicate a song for you, for you are very special to me. "Airplane without wings, fire without wood, it is like me without you. Soccer without ball, Tweety without Sylvester, it is like me without you. Why has it to be this way? My desire has no end. I want you all the time, a thousand speaker will not be able to speak for me. I don't exist far away from you and loneliness is my worst punishment, I count the hours to see you, but the clock seems not to like me." This song I have chosen to send you, I like it very much, I have danced it on Mother's Day.

I am very proud of you, every day I thank God for putting you on my way and because you have been a blessing for me and my family.

I thank you for the beautiful letter and photos you sent me. I am so glad you write to me. It is so good! You are a blessing for me and you are an angel.

I am so happy that you come to visit me. I dream to give you a big hug. May God continue blessings you and you grow in your minister each day. And God's glory shines like sun in you.

You are very special to me. Thanks for your lovely letters. I love hearing from you. I will keep praying for all of you. Stay strong and trust in the Lord always. How many sponsored children do you help? I know God will reward your generosity.

At the project I have a very good teacher, and she said that you are an angel sent by God to me. I agree with her, for me and for all the kids. Thanks for sponsoring me, and I know that all the kids are blessed by you are very happy.

I was very happy to get your letter and I love to listen to all the words you write me. David, thank you for your prayers, it has been helping me a lot. I am glad to know that there is someone who loves me so much. May God bless your life always and may you be happy. I look forward to receive other letter from you, they make me very well, it is a way to have you closer to me.

How It Started for Me

In October 2006 I attended the Willow Creek Global Leadership Summit at Kardinia Church in Geelong with a group of people from the church I was attending at the time. One of the presentations was an interview between Bill Hybels and Bono from the rock band U2. I am a huge U2 fan, so this was the part I was looking forward to. It was an enjoyable interview in which Bono took his usual swipes at the institution of the local church and encouraged us to *do* something to combat the evils of the world.

At the time, God had been challenging me in regards to the way I used what He had given me to help others, even though I was a university student living off government welfare money. I don't remember what it was about the Bono conversation that prompted me, but that day I decided to sponsor a child. I had sponsored with other organizations in the past but it had been a largely impersonal and unrewarding experience.

Compassion had a stand at the back of the venue and I approached them and started looking at the child packets, which contain each child's photo and basic information. I chose 5-year-old Daila from Colombia, mainly because her birthday is close to mine. I actually thought I was sponsoring from Cambodia (I knew about the landmines) but when I realized my error it didn't matter, since Colombia has some pretty serious problems of its own.

And that's where the Compassion journey began.

Journey #1—Bolivia, Colombia, El Salvador 2009

What follows are the accounts of my personal Compassion travels: 31 children visited in 12 countries.

During the first two years of the sponsorship journey, there was something about the way Compassion worked that just grabbed me. In 2008 I started working full-time as a teacher. I had a Grade 1/2 class at a little country school and they enthusiastically jumped on board with me. I showed them pictures of the kids and we wrote them letters. It was important for them to see that not all kids live like they do and they should be thankful for what they have. The full-time job brought a massive increase in my income. Rather than stockpile all this extra money up for myself, I made the intentional decision to use it to help others and by 2009 I was sponsoring six kids.

Unlike some other child development organizations, Compassion believes that the best way to allay any skepticism, doubts or fears a person has about the value of child sponsorship is to go and visit their child. They actively encourage it and even organize group tours, where you get an inside look at all Compassion's programs. In 2009 I decided to see for myself and organized an individual trip to visit three of my kids: Sehila in Bolivia, Daila in Colombia (on my birthday) and Rosa in El Salvador.

Visiting Sehila in Bolivia
Tuesday 29 September 2009
The first stop was to visit Sehila (pronounced 'Shay-la') in Bolivia. I arrived in La Paz early in the morning and met my translator in the hotel lobby. Sehila came in soon after. She was ten years old and in Grade Five at school. We shared a nice big hug and I met her father Reynaldo, who was a driver. Unfortunately Sehila's mother and sisters were away, taking their grandmother to have eye surgery, so I didn't get to meet them. Five of us then piled into a taxi to go to Compassion Project BO-433 where

Sehila was registered (*she and her family have since moved to a different area*).

Sehila was quite shy but coped pretty well with the language barrier that existed between us. She took a real shine to the soft toy koala I gave her, which didn't surprise me. I broke the ice somewhat by making her laugh a few times and told her about some Australian animals. The saddest part was when I told her the ten or so words I could speak in Spanish, and she still couldn't understand me!!

The Compassion Project had been operating for two years, had 210 children attending, and at that time had two toilets in the whole place. I met all the staff (one male), a couple of whom could speak English, and had a tour of the Project. There are several classrooms, a common room where they eat, and a church up the top. It was interesting that they said Sehila wasn't too sure whether I'd actually come–I'm glad I didn't let her down.

The children come to the Project in the early afternoon, after school finishes. They are in an area where the majority of the children go to school. They are grouped with others of similar age, with whom they do classes, homework, learn about spiritual things and play games. There is also a meal waiting for them when they first arrive.

The first time I went to the Project in the morning, the children weren't there because they were still in school, so this gave me a chance to chat to the staff. I was informed that I was the second sponsor visit to the Project. They made me a cake which was really nice, and they basically sat around and watched me eat it. As a gift they gave me a pen and a 'Bolivia' pen holder with an engraving on the back.

After spending some time at the Project we left to walk to Sehila's house, which wasn't too far away. This gave me a chance to observe the local neighborhood. Lots of mangy stray dogs and rubbish on the streets. The 'roads,' if you could call them that, were incredibly under-made, pot-holey and rough as guts. Some of the local roads were undergoing redevelopment so there were piles of rocks and stones just sitting there, presumably waiting for a bulldozer to come and smooth them out.

I wasn't sure what I expected Sehila's house to be like, so I wasn't shocked or surprised at what I saw. Her father had recently paid for the house for two years (I guess like either a 'long term rent' or 'short term buy' agreement), so that gave the family some stability. The house had a small concrete yard protected by a fence. They had an outdoor enclosed toilet and shower (like an outhouse) and three rooms–kitchen, dining room/lounge. There was one bedroom for the family which was very neat and well lit–one double bed for the parents, and one for the three girls. The kitchen had a stove, an oven and a sink with running water. They had a TV and a couple of couches. Sehila had a fair soft toy collection, including a Kermit the frog!

She showed me lots of photos of her family, mainly of her parents when they were younger, and a few of her and her sisters. The weather was cold all day and while we were in Sehila's house it started to rain, then hail for a while, so we were stuck inside.

Unfortunately there were some awkward silences, firstly because I found myself having to drive the conversations, which I'm not good at doing in the first place, and in addition I was struggling a fair bit with the language barrier. So we sat for a while, which was excruciating, because it wasn't 'supposed to' happen. I, having come all that way, should have had lots of things to say, lots of questions to ask etc. It should have been one happy gathering. But it wasn't like that much of the time.

Once it stopped raining we got a cab back to the Project, where by this time the rest of the children had arrived and were eating their lunch. All eyes turned toward me as I entered the room…silence…then I shouted one of the few Spanish words I knew – "*Hola*!!" and gave a big wave. The children responded and quite a few of them rushed toward me and squashed me in a big hug. Unfortunately due to my limited Spanish all I could say was "*Como estas*?" and that was really as far as the interaction went.

We had lunch in the same room as the kids—rice, potatoes and some sort of spicy cow meat. Some of the older kids came over and started talking to me (via my translator of course), asking me lots of questions about 'my country' and I asked them lots of questions about 'their country.' We learned a lot and had a good chat.

After lunch they lined up, I introduced myself and taught them about a few Australian animals. I had them jumping like a kangaroo, snoring and climbing like a koala, and running like an emu. Some of the younger kids were off on another planet so I just stopped. I was surprised how hard it seemed to be for the children to copy what I said. When I tried to get them to say things like 'kangaroo', 'koala', 'wombat', they really struggled. I thought they were just sounds, no matter what language you speak them in. Oh well.

I then spent a bit of time in Sehila's classroom, seeing the sorts of activities they did and how they interacted. I learned that Bolivian kids are just like Australian kids, and just because they go to the Compassion Project it doesn't make them angels, saints, or perfect well-behaved children (noted when a couple of the older boys started fighting in the classroom).

Around mid-afternoon I started feeling pretty tired (I had been on a plane through the previous night), so I struggled with the possibility of leaving. I had thought I would be trying to eke out every possible minute I could with Sehila, not wanting to go at all, having to be dragged away. The reality was we had spent six hours together and I had seen into every area of her life about as comprehensively as I could. There was probably not much to be gained by hanging around as she went about her normal life, so I got a couple more photos with her, said goodbye to the Project director and left.

Visiting Daila in Colombia
Thursday 1 October 2009
On October 1st (my birthday) I was up at 5am for the trip from Cali to Buenaventura, on the west coast of Colombia. I met my translator, host and taxi driver. As we travelled I could tell we were pretty high up, partly

because the clouds seemed like they were just above us, and also my ears were popping. The mountains and the scenery were breathtaking, and at the same time, the poverty we passed was indescribable. It is a cliché, but it was indeed just like on TV. The people who live in the mountains are either farmers or make their living with roadside stalls. Houses are clumsily put together with whatever materials people can get their hands on. Horses are commonly used for transport, since they cannot all afford cars. The drive was interesting. Pesky motorbikes, annoying slow trucks, near-collisions every five minutes and people just overtaking whenever they felt like it.

We got pulled over at a police checkpoint and a cop went through every inch of all my luggage, especially the toy koala I had. Naturally everything was fine and apparently it was 'normal', but it was still a bit unnerving. After a two-and-a-half hour drive, at 8.30am we arrived at Buenaventura, which consists of 80% people of African descent, so of course I got my fair share of stares from people as we passed by.

Our first stop was Project CO-437 which had 250 children at the time, and met the staff, the Pastor of the church, and Daila's family. Daila has three siblings: two sisters Daniela and Luisa, and a brother Jorge. Daila's father was the same age as me, and was very friendly and chatty. If I had known Spanish, we would be best buddies! In contrast, her mother didn't say a word. She designs things like jewelry and bags, and had made me a knitted bag with 'Colombia' written on it, with some bracelets inside as a gift. I wore it around the whole time I was there.

First we had breakfast and some of the Project kids performed songs and dances that they had practised. At the end of one of the dances they crowded together, and came up to me to reveal…Daila! I totally didn't see it coming. Daila was quite shy but she was also very affectionate.

Next we visited Daila's house, which was only five minutes from the Project. The family lived in a very poor neighborhood and the house was basically one room, with a section sealed off for the parents' bedroom.

Unimaginable for a family of six, but that's the reality in this area. It is the house Daila's father grew up in and now her grandfather lives in a hut out the back.

After having a chat we saw Daila's school, which was two minutes down the road. We met the Principal, who was also the Pastor's wife. I learned that when they want to start a school they don't build, they just look for available houses and turn them into a school. After this we went back to the Project, where the kids sang 'Happy Birthday' to me as I entered and presented me with a cake. We sat down and ate the cake, then went on a tour of the Project. There wasn't much to see really, just two rooms and an eating area. I was able to have a look at Daila's information folder, which was very comprehensive, to see the 'behind the scenes' stuff that Compassion does to ensure the well-being of each child.

We then saw the church which is connected to the Project and I jumped on the drums and had a play. People were peering in from the street to see who was making all the noise. The church was in the process of building an extra room on the property in order to extend the capabilities of the Project.

Finally we walked back the Project and had lunch, which was a traditional Colombian dish called 'Buanga.' It went down a treat! Then I entertained the kids for a while with a finger trick, thumb wars and paper scissors rock. Early in the afternoon it was time to go. I had a great time.

We were going to drive around Buenaventura for a while before we left but apparently there was some sort of protest or demonstration happening in town which had the potential to get ugly, so we just headed back to Cali. On the way it started to rain, which added an extra element of adventure. Unsurprisingly we were stopped by the police and searched again on the way back.

Michael, my translator for the day, said something that really meant a lot to me. He said he was very impressed with what I was doing, sponsoring six children, and when he started earning his own income he was going to sponsor a child because he had seen the impact it had through my visit, and I had inspired him. How good is that? I'd known this young guy for only a few hours and I inspired him! All in all, a great way to spend a birthday.

Visiting Rosa in El Salvador

Saturday 3 October 2009

Finally it was time to visit Rosa in El Salvador. On my flight to San Salvador I sat next to a Peruvian couple, Luis and Carmen. Carmen could speak acceptable English but Luis knew very little. Carmen had lots of sheets with English-Spanish vocabulary and I ended up teaching her how to pronounce many English words. We ended up chatting and I found out they were headed to the US to visit some friends and maybe work. I told them about the sponsor child adventure I was on and they came to the conclusion that I must be either a priest or a missionary. That really meant a lot to me– these two people I'd only just met were so impacted by what I was doing, they immediately thought of the two big 'Christian' occupations.

This day started a bit later than the others. I was picked up by Carlos my translator and John my driver at 7.30am on a warm and sticky day, to head to Chinameca which was about two and a half hours away. The drive was a lot different to Bolivia and Colombia. The roads were high quality and paved, and the drivers were a lot more civil. Chinameca is out toward the east of El Salvador where most people are farmers, therefore quite poor, and you could see it as we got further from the city.

An interesting fact about San Miguel: because it is close to the border with Honduras, it is the place of choice for 'contraband.' Now the most popular contraband is not what you would usually expect, but it is milk and cheese. Because El Salvadorians produce so little but consume so much, the people try and smuggle it in to avoid having to pay the high taxes on it.

We arrived at Project ES-718 at about 9.30am and I was amazed to see about 100 children lined up outside with Australian flags! Normally there are no Project activities on a Saturday but my visit had also coincided with their national Children's Day, so everyone was very festive and excited.

We met altogether in the church. The kids sang some songs, I introduced myself and met Rosa and her family. Dad, Mum, older stepsister Vanesa, brother Josue and twin sister Ester. They gave me some gifts–a plaque with Psalm 91 in Spanish, a scarf that Rosa had knitted herself and an album with lots of photos of Rosa.

We took a tour of the Project, which is truly an oasis in a neighborhood that is not really child-friendly–same old story but sad reality for these kids. Carlos told me that at that time El Salvador had 160 Projects with 35,000 sponsored kids. I saw the classroom that Rosa learns about God in, then we watched the kids playing games and whacking piñatas, and I had an amusing English teaching session with some of the kids where I would point to a body part or object, get them to say it in 'Espanol' and I would teach them the English word. It was quite hilarious listening to them mimic my Australian accent.

A real treat was being able to take the whole family to Pizza Hut in San Miguel. Normally sponsors only take the child and one parent, but paying $55 for 10 people to share this experience was really a small price to pay, so I was happy to do it. A highlight was having the staff come and sing me their birthday song, as our crew had told them it was my birthday a couple of days ago.

After this we visited the Hernandez family house. It had belonged to Rosa's grandfather and he passed it on to his son. Once again, it was basically one room with curtains used as dividers, for six people. This wasn't necessarily surprising to me but was still confronting to see the conditions that a family of six was living in. However, they seemed relatively content and thankful to God for providing their needs.

When we arrived at the house it was like the family had known me my whole life, as they handed round nice cold cans of Coke!! We toured the house, saw their dog, cat, chickens and birds, including a green Australian parakeet. Finally it came to say goodbye. For some reason I found parting harder on this occasion than the other two visits. I don't know why, but the best I can come up with is there was just something about this family that I felt attached to, and I did get a lump in the throat at the end.

Carlos had some nice words when we chatted at the end. He brought up something I said in a previous conversation about recognizing I've been blessed by God so I want to pass those blessings on. He read 1 Chronicles 29:10-14

> *David praised the LORD in the presence of the whole assembly, saying…*
> *"Yours, O LORD, is the greatness and the power and the glory and the victory and the majesty. Everything in heaven and on earth is yours and this is your kingdom…riches and honor come from you alone, for you ruler over everything. Power and might are in your hands and it is at yur discretion that people are made great and given strength..*
> *Now, our God, we give you thanks, and praise your glorious name.*
> *"But who am I, and who are my people, that we could give anything to you? Everything we have comes from you, and we give you only what you have already given us."*

This summed up my attitude perfectly. Who am I, that God would use me in such an amazing way? Trust me dear reader: if He can use me, He can use anyone!

The Crazy Compassion Plan and
The Divine Economy, 2011

I want to share with you a story about what I call 'The Divine Economy.' It's very clear from the Bible that God wants those of us who have much to share what we have with those who don't have much. It just makes sense. Here are a couple of verses I love, which illustrate this.

Proverbs 11:24 says *"It is possible to give freely, yet become more wealthy, but those who are stingy will lose everything."*.

In Proverbs 19:17 we read *"If you help the poor, you are lending to the Lord-and He will repay you!"*

I want you to know that God and His Word are true, and I am living proof of these verses.

The story I'm about to share happened to me in 2011 and I want to make it clear that I don't intend to sound like I'm boasting in myself. I'm not that foolish, and I know that everything I have and everything I am comes from God.

At the start of 2011 I sponsored seven children with Compassion. I had a nice little secure full-time teaching job at a Lutheran School and I felt like God was encouraging me to do more. I got this thought in my head: *"Imagine the impact it could have if I sponsored at least one child from all 26 countries Compassion works in."* I called it my 'Crazy Compassion Plan', and over the course of the year I put that plan into action. By the end of the year I had sponsored 40 children, from 26 countries.

Keeping in mind the above promises from The Good Word, during the year the following things happened:
*   Soon after I sponsored ten more kids, I was paid an extra $400 a week by my school for supervising a group of bus travelers before

and after school (*almost the exact amount of my sponsorships at that time*).

* I started up after-school music lessons and my number of students increased at the same time my Compassion family increased.
* I made the intentional decision to become debt-free and was able to pay off a five-figure car loan as well as my University loan.
* I ended up with more money in the bank at the end of the year than I had at the start.

That, my friends, is called the *Divine Economy*. It makes no sense in the 'commonsensical,' scientific, natural world. Normally, the more you spend, the less you have. However, what God taught me through this year is that if you 'give freely and receive loosely,' with a generous heart and for the benefit of others, God will provide for you. I am proof of that.

And once again, none of this happened *because* of me. God, in His grace and mercy, chose to provide for me in this way because He is true to His Word and His promises. Why not give it a go?

Brazil Journey #1-September/October 2012

Brazil. The experiences, adventures and lessons I've learned from my time in Brazil over the last couple of years could honestly fill their own book. Due to the dire family situation of my sponsored child Ana Cristina (mentioned at the start of the book), God caused my heart to ache for Brazil above all other places. I have visited Fortaleza twice to see the work of God through Compassion despite so many barriers and obstacles, and it is magnificent.

Their home lives are unimaginably hard but what I witnessed at the Compassion Projects seriously warmed my heart: enthusiastic and joyful kids singing, dancing, learning, feeling loved and safe, talented teenagers playing instruments and planning community events. Because of God and Compassion, they've been infused with Hope and their lives reflect this. Some highlights: "Dancing" with Marta. Playing guitar with John and drums with Tereza. Meeting my sponsored kids, including now-graduated Monalisa and Alynne. Eating cotton candy with Camis. Frantically searching for power adaptors with my translators Isabela and Anderson. Touring Fortaleza with Debora. Hearing the amazing stories of Compassion graduates Lucas, Hosana, Rafaele, Carol and Livia.

Best of all I was able to share the simple joys and experiences of a birthday party (mine, twice!) with kids and adults who I may never meet again in this life, but through our brief connection we both got a taste of the love of God and none of us will ever be the same again. Thank you Brazil for your faith, joy and kindness.

What follows is the accounts of my visits to Brazil.

More about Ana Cristina
As I mentioned at the start of the book, my first sponsored child from Brazil was Ana Cristina. She also happened to be the first child I'd sponsored who was smiling in their profile picture. I did not plan it that

way, but this only became significant to me when I learned more about her life and community.

Cristina lives in Fortaleza, which I understand is one of the worst places in the world for child prostitution and the related evil that comes with it. She is one of six children and her mother was 13 when she gave birth to her oldest child, Cristina's older brother. I received a letter from the Pastor of Cristina's church, giving details about the community. They are surrounded by a dried up river full of untreated sewage and effluent on one side, and a swamp on the other, which leaves them at risk of flooding when it rains. Because of this there is no industry or commerce, which means there are no jobs, which means there is high unemployment, alcoholism, violence, drugs, gambling, unstructured families... Hell on earth basically.

It was then that I looked at Cristina and wondered: "*How does a person manage to smile while living in those circumstances?*" I am still at a loss to answer that, but my guess would be that that person has the hope of the love of God and trusts Him to provide for their needs. In Cristina's case, this hope comes from the help of Compassion.

After grasping that this was the reality for this child and her family, God moved my heart and I sponsored six more children from Brazil, all from the same Project which is also in Fortaleza.

In August 2011, I received a letter from Ana Cristina's tutor saying that Cristina's uncle had been killed, and they had moved away for a while. I desperately lifted her up to God in prayer for two weeks and one morning I received an email with Cristina's name in the subject line. This is what I read:

Hi David,
My name is Hayley and I work for Compassion Australia.

Two weeks ago my husband and I visited our sponsor boy in Fortaleza, Brazil and also another Compassion project in the area—BR458.

Throughout the course of the day, one of the young girls at the project came up to me and shyly through the translator showed me the letter her sponsor wrote her. She said her sponsor was from Australia. I took a photo of her holding her sponsor letter.

Upon returning home and investigating further, I have discovered it was in fact your little sponsor girl Cristina! I attach some photos of beautiful Ana Cristina and her project and hope that you enjoy!

It was such an amazing experience to visit her project (BR458). In fact, it was one of the highlights of our four week holiday! The community that Cristina, Rocy and Jessica live in is fairly horrific. Raw sewage runs through the streets, there is no electricity and worse, houses are small and fairly ramshackle and worse, there are a lot of people that have no hope. Drugs are a huge problem in fact, one of the boys in the project has recently lost his father in a drug debt related murder.

In the community, the children are taught that they were born poor, they will die poor. In the project, they learn that they are valued, that God has a purpose for their life, and that they can dream big. They go home with aspirations of becoming a doctor, or a teacher–in a community where playing cards and drinking at 11am on a Monday morning is normal practice... Then, as they change, they start to change their parent's attitudes. As a result parents are giving up drugs, trying to find work and some are even giving their life to Christ. To see and hear about this project first hand was just miraculous – God is at work! And - the project staff are amazing! The project director is also the church pastor, he attends the project 5 days a week and just does life with the kids, does pastoral care in the community, writes sermons for Sunday mornings (where the church has grown from 12 to 120!) and somehow finds the time to do large jig-saw puzzles which he then raffles off to raise money for the project and the church! His love and the love of the other staff towards the children was palpable – I was blown away!

I just felt the project was such a beacon in the community. There, the children were able to be children! They were joyful, hopeful and happy.

I couldn't stop smiling for about a week! I was so grateful for God's grace and mercy in this situation, and He continually reminds me that as much as I love these kids, He loves them more and has His hand on their lives.

Visiting BR-458, Projeto Sementinhas (Little Seeds) and Home Visits
Thursday 27 September 2012

At the start of 2012 I organized a trip for late September to visit my nine sponsored kids in Brazil. I sponsored three kids at BR-458 (Cristina, Jessica and Christian) and six at BR-110. During the year, two of the kids from BR-110 left the Compassion program for different reasons so, with the help of my friend and fellow advocate Beverly Yearwood, I arranged to sponsor three more from Project BR-329 (Monalisa, Alynne and Larissa) in the knowledge that I would visit them in a couple of months. This was definitely a 'God-thing'.

The plan for the trip was to spend a few days visiting homes and Projects, and then on my birthday I wanted to treat them all to a special day at a Park. I was inspired to do this by Angela and Nabi Saleh, who are the co-founders of Gloria Jeans Coffee. A few years ago they threw a huge pool party for their 250-ish sponsored kids in Brazil and I thought it would be great to do a similar thing, albeit on a smaller scale.

As time went on, I decided to invite all the caregivers and siblings as well (close to 50 people) however much it cost me, because I was sure God was going to do something magnificent in all our lives on this day.

The trip finally came around, and I am certain I will never plan a trip nine months in advance ever again! Compassion Project BR-458, Projeto Sementinhas (Little Seeds Project) was the first stop. I felt like I knew the place because Hayley, the Compassion employee who had visited that Project previously, sent me videos and photos. It is located in the region of Caucaia, just outside Fortaleza. Here I sponsored Ana Cristina (12), Jessica (8) and Christian (8).

The Project had been running for five years and had 152 children. Pastor Josue actually began caring for neighborhood kids before he joined with Compassion. He started with seven kids, increased to 20-something and then found out about Compassion. When they met, Compassion encouraged him to get 100 kids before forming a partnership. The Project has three classrooms and is relatively new.

The new church was being built on site, so the kids main play area was basically a construction zone. They played in bare feet and flip-flops and had to contend with dirt, rocks, stones, and possibly nails and glass. OH&S boffins would be horrified! Fortunately Pastor Josue lives just across the road and he provides them with a safer place to play.

I'll be honest. In my mind I went through what I hoped meeting these kids would be like, probably a thousand times over, and the way it went down was, initially, an anti-climax. All three of them were in their classes and when I went in there I almost felt like I was interrupting things. We took them downstairs to have a get-to-know-you chat and didn't get much out of them. They were just shy, withdrawn and overwhelmed. Cristina and Jessica stayed that way for the majority of the day but Christian was by far the most open and expressive of the three.

Another interesting thing was how little they knew or remembered about me, despite the fact that I sent them letters and pictures at least once a month, of at least one page in length. I don't hold back in my letters. They should have basically known my life story. I don't know whether it's a translation issue, but I thought they should have known more than they did.

Isabela and I did a good job of keeping things moving, and soon enough the other kids came down for their snack. I got lots of curious looks and shy glances. I stuck my hand out for a high five to see who would get it. Some did, others walked right past. After the snack it was music time! They performed a couple of songs for me and I taught them a couple of songs I learned as a summer camp counsellor in Indiana back in 2004. It was good they were mainly action songs because the language barrier proved a bit tricky.

After this we had some free time out in the construction zone/half built church. They loved to play a game that was similar to dodge-ball, but as a way of keeping everyone in the game, if you got hit you go up one end and continue playing. I also taught them paper-scissors-rock, thumb-wars, a finger trick and 'My Aunty Anna' (a hand-clapping game where the person who can slide their legs apart the furthest wins).

This group of kids were very receptive and curious. We had to deal with the language barrier, but all I had to do was walk with a wiggle and I had them in stitches.

Another special event I was able to be part of today was giving some gifts to a child from their sponsor all the way from the United States. I met Jennifer Nunley on the OurCompassion website, which is like a social networking site for Compassion sponsors, and she sponsors Erica from this Project. When she found out I was going there she was keen to send some gifts. The Project staff very kindly arranged for Erica to be at the Project on this day, and I was able to meet her, give her the gifts, as well as take some photos and video to give to Jennifer.

One thing that went down really well was the Australian football I brought along. This group of kids really got into it, especially my boy Christian, who carried it round with him when we went walking on the home visits. I taught them how to kick and handball, then we played some kick-to-kick for a while. They even had to be encouraged to go back to their soccer game–they'd forgotten all about it!

I was looked after really well. Once again the hospitality was fantastic and the Project staff genuinely care about the kids they've been entrusted with and any visitors that may come. They are truly being the hands and feet of Jesus.

Lesson learned: On this day I learned that God is a God who answers prayers, whether or not it comes in the form we want or expect. Before this trip I repeatedly prayed for God to clothe me in humility and to help me remember that this is all about Him. There was not one occasion on this first day for me to get a big head. There was no great outpouring of emotion or gratitude from any of the kids or parents, even though I know they loved having me there and were appreciative of all I've done. They were just very low-key in the way they expressed it.

BR-458 Home visits – Jessica and Christian

For the two home visits we were joined by all three kids, plus Jessica's sister Juliana. One thing I *loved* seeing was the way the four of them interacted with each other. We had a 15-minute walk to each house in baking heat, through unpaved and dangerous streets with rubbish and sewage everywhere, stray cats and dogs running around and motorbikes whizzing past. I marveled at how they wandered along, seemingly without a care in the world, chatting and laughing with each other and Christian playing with (and frequently dropping) the football.

Cristina took on a bit of a mother role, reminding the others to stay to the side of the road if they strayed too far to the middle. It was particularly precious seeing Jessica and Cristina walking along holding hands, and during the home visits Jessica would sit on Cristina's lap. It was a relief to me to see that there was not a hint of jealousy or competition between the kids. This showed me that they were secure in the knowledge that I loved them the same.

Jessica lives with her mother, father, older sister Juliana and baby brother Pedro. Her mother earns a living by stitching and embroidering patterns on bras and underwear. There were several boxes full around the house, so she must be busy. She is able to work from home, so this helps her look after the baby. Their living conditions are simple and basic.

The family has a dog and a cat. They are joined in surrounding houses by relatives and extended family. We were joined on our visit by five or six young cousins, some only in their underwear, which at a guess was probably not by choice. Jessica seemed quiet and shy, but also cheerful and sweet.

Next stop was Christian's house. He was a great little guy and was definitely the most open and expressive of the three. He radiated excitement and energy. He *loved* the Australian football. When we went to his house he showed it to his relatives and they scratched their heads and just stared at it for about 20 seconds.

I also taught him the correct way to say 'footy', that is, 'oo' as in book and pronounce the 't' as a 'd', so it becomes 'foody'. He kept saying it over and over again–classic! One thing I noticed was he was very receptive to the things of God and the Bible. When we were at Jessica's house, they were asked what their favorite Bible story was, and 8-year-old Christian came out with Jesus and the Samaritan woman at the well, and proceeded to recount it! That's a pretty deep favorite Bible story for a child.

Christian is an only child, and up until recently lived with his mother, grandparents and uncle–not exactly a 'nuclear' family. However, apparently just the previous week his mother got married to his father and they moved into their own house. I hoped this would lead to a stable home environment for Christian to grow up in.

Christian's grandpa had injured his hand/wrist/arm after being hit by a car, and it was all curled up so his hand was pointing to the sky. They told us that the driver was never brought to justice. I could tell this wounded them because it prevented him from working and earning a much-needed income.

Christian's mother made money by collecting recyclable materials and selling them on to a guy. She didn't have set work hours but just found and collected things wherever she was going. One of the walls of the grandparent's house was piled high with plastic bottles waiting to be resold.

We weren't able to visit Ana Cristina's house, because they live in a different area due to her family's situation. The area she lived in at this time did not have a Compassion Project. Normally she would be forced to depart the program but they have made an exception for this family because of the relationship I formed with her through sponsorship and because of the visit. I learned that the family were just about to pull her out, then they found out I was visiting and decided to let her keep coming! That blew me away and made me feel so humble and thankful.

Sponsors: It is worth putting extra time and effort into writing to and praying for your kids! You never know what can happen as a result.

Visiting BR-110 Espaco Esperanca (Hope Space Project) and Home Visits
Friday 28 September 2012

What an incredible day! Our day started with a scavenger hunt. I had foolishly forgotten to bring a power adapter, and evidently they're as rare as hen's teeth in Brazil, so my wonderful translator Isabela went well above and beyond the call of duty to try and find me one. Our search led us to downtown Fortaleza and it was like a gauntlet! Cars, bikes, motorbikes, trolleys, carts and people all fought for a tiny space of road. On one occasion Isabela parked and left the engine running while she went from shop to shop. Eventually my nerves got the better of me and I turned the engine off. Imagine finding a running car with a foreigner in the passenger seat? Jackpot!

We arrived at the Project and I met the girls: Taina (7) Pamella (9), Alice (8) and Ana Alice (8) (pronounced Ana-lee-see). We took a photo in front of a sign that said *"David–Your presence fills us with joy!"*

Our first stop was the music class. John Nascimento is a former sponsored child of this Project and he is now studying as a student of the Leadership Development Program. He's also back at the Project teaching music and has recorded a CD of Brazilian guitar music with five other guys. The boys in the music class performed, then I was invited to play something. Funnily enough I 'just happened' to bring music for a couple of songs. I played and sang the worship song 'Forever' and John, being the talented guy he is, played along. The girls then sang a song and we moved on to a short tour of the Project.

BR-110 is one of Brazil's most established Projects. It's been around for about 25 years and you can tell. The classrooms are bigger, there are more of them, and they have a nice big undercover play area. Music and dance are integral classes and they have a garden where they grow vegetables, both for the Project and the community. The Projects also sometimes compete in sporting and music competitions in the community and BR-110 had a fair collection of trophies.

Today was a planning day for the staff so there were very few kids around. We were joined by Ana Alice's sister Camila as well as a couple of boys from the Project. While we were at the Project we did some painting and drawing (correction: they painted and drew while I watched), played some hide and seek and they showed me some dances they'd been practising. I taught them some silly fun songs. The language barrier made it hard but we managed.

I also brought the Australian football along again. Most of them had a little turn but they were probably a bit young. Camila and the two boys were right into it though, and we had a nice big space to play. One of the gifts they gave me was a t-shirt with the girl's faces on it but on the caption they had written 'United States' instead of 'Australia'. Whoops! I didn't hold it against them.

BR-110 Home visits–Pamella and Alice
We were only able to visit two of the four houses today because some of the parents were working. It was disappointing, but there was not much we could do about it. So we were off on a walking tour of the streets of Brazil to the houses of Alice and Pamella. Once again it was a fair eye opener and I was way out of my comfort zone.

The neighborhoods of all three Projects felt very similar, at least to me. I felt eyes on me wherever we went. There was sewage running down the streets, people lying in doorways, houses were covered in bars and padlocks, putting anything of value on display was a no-no. And yet having said all that, the kids just laughed, chatted and skipped all the way along.

The common status symbol on the streets seemed to be unnecessarily massive speakers which were put on the back of motor bikes or on top of cars and pumped up way *past* 11 on the volume dial, so periodically we'd be walking or talking and we'd receive a cerebral blast of Portuguese something-or-other. Having made their point, whatever it was, the car or motor bike in question would proudly move along.

We were a motley crew: me, Isabela, Ezir (Project staff member), the four girls, Camila and an older boy from the Project. Every so often I would look around and just laugh about the absurdity of where I had found myself. I never imagined in my wildest dreams I would be walking the streets of Brazil. *Following God takes you to some strange places, but He's always there with you.*

First stop was Pamella's house. Nine-year-old Pamella was clearly the leader of the four-girl pack. She is also a larger girl, and I believe this has an effect on the way she sees herself. She is an absolute sweetheart and never short of a word but what really stood out to me was a massive need for affirmation, approval and love. Her emotional tank seemed so empty and her insecurity shone like a beacon. When she was painting something for me she started again three or four times because it 'wasn't good enough.' She even made random negative comments to Isabela about her own body and personality. This made my heart ache for her.

Pamella lives with her godmother and godfather who care for her very much. She does have parents and siblings but they live somewhere else. The reason for this wasn't mentioned. The godparents have a daughter who Pamella calls her aunt.

The aunt is 18 and is off working in Portugal, though it wasn't mentioned what she is doing. She periodically sends money back to the family, and for this reason certain parts of Pamella's house are nicer and more modern than many of the other houses in the area. However because the money being sent is not regular, the family still falls under Compassion's economic profile. The godfather is a taxi driver and popped in to say hello while we were visiting.

Next stop, not too far away, was Alice's house. Alice was sort of stuck in the middle of the group. Personality-wise she is sweet but quiet and I get the feeling she is easily overshadowed. Living in a household of nine people will do that to you I guess. There were an assortment of siblings and cousins around the place and we noticed they held a healthy devotion to a TV show called 'Rebelde.' There were posters and pictures up on walls and in frames and Alice was able to rattle off the characters like a pro.

I was told there was a possibility Taina may be released from the Compassion program but was still in it at the time because of her home situation. Her father left the family for a while but now he has returned. He works in construction and makes enough to help the family without Compassion's assistance, however I was told he is quite volatile and is apparently sometimes prone to physical violence. So because Compassion is holistic in their care of the child, a child will not be released from the program simply because their family makes enough money. The Compassion staff look at all areas of their life and if one area is at risk, they prefer to look after them.

What really made today a joy is that, at least on the surface, there didn't seem to be much between the girls in the way of jealousy or competition for my attention. I made sure I talked to and played with each of them and they seemed to get along well.

Visiting BR-329 Centro Estudantil Vida Nova (New Life Student Center) and Home Visits
Saturday 29 September 2012

I could *never* have imagined the impact that the third Project visit would have on my life. The first two days had been amazing, but I had no idea that God had even more incredible things in store for me. I had only been sponsoring Larissa, Monalisa and Alynne for four months and we hadn't yet exchanged letters.

Four-year-old Larissa was very shy and not even a teddy bear could help her warm to me. I did get a smile out of her–when it was time to go! I also met 17-year-old Alynne, who took me on a tour of the Project and I was able to visit her house. She hopes to be a lawyer. 18-year-old Monalisa was in a wheelchair, having broken her leg three weeks before the visit. She hopes to be a vet. Monalisa and Alynne have now graduated from the Compassion program.

The visit to BR-329 was on a Saturday, and the place was full of teenagers, busy, welcoming and curious. It is an urban Project and serves about 680 kids with minimal space. We went into the main area and waiting for me was a 15-piece band. This wasn't just your normal guitar/bass/drum band, but they had flutes, clarinets, trumpets, saxophones and even a tuba!!

Something you should know about me is that music is a major part of who I am. I have taught it at school, I play drums, bass, guitar, keyboard and I sing. God has 'ingrained' music into my soul, and there's nothing I'd rather be doing than playing drums or bass guitar.

The band played a couple of songs for us, including one in particular that had a nice little funky Brazilian beat to it (pity I can't dance, but more about that soon), then I was introduced and asked to pray for the group. It looked as though they were about to be sent off to their classes so I quickly mentioned to Isabela that I'd like the chance to get on the drums at some stage during the day (hint hint). She talked to the director and they invited me to play a song with them. It was truly a highlight of my life–a talented band, and at least 50 Brazilian teenagers going nuts and dancing away. I just loved the whole atmosphere and I never miss a chance to 'show off' my drumming.

After I got off the drums they played a couple of other songs and set up a dance floor (NO!). I wished I could have made myself invisible at this point, but I couldn't. Straight away a couple of girls came over and wanted to dance. I reluctantly accepted, quickly proved my incompetence in this area and skulked away laughing, apologetic and embarrassed. They were very forgiving.

I felt like I'd walked into a little piece of heaven among the poverty and danger that existed outside the walls of the Project. I experienced pure and genuine life, joy, hope, peace, music and dancing. The Compassion staff have huge dreams and vision, including a massive two-story building extension, and trust God for everything. Their gratitude for my visit, and even my life, was overwhelming and humbling.

A few of the girls asked me to pose for photos and they went off to their classes. At this point I sat down with my three sponsored girls and Isabela and we had a conversation to get to know each other better. I explained why I had only sent them one letter to that point (because I only sponsored them a couple of months ago and knew I was coming to visit, so by the time I sent another letter it would arrive after the visit), but I made up for it by printing out every letter from 2012 that I had sent my other kids, as well as about 20 pages of photos – someone had a lot of translating to do!

Each of the girls had made me a birthday card with a sweet message on it (which I also had to get translated). After this, Monalisa stayed put in her wheelchair while Alynne took me round on a tour of the Project. It is an urban Project that serves 680 kids, as well as another 200 or so who are part of a government youth program. Many Compassion Projects and churches open up their facilities to outside community groups, which is the best way to gain the trust and confidence of parents and others, rather than just remaining a closed shop.

The Project staff are forced to be economical with the way they use their space–most classrooms are used for two or three different activities during the week. However, at the time they had a two-storey building extension happening. When it is complete they will be able to have all activities on the one property. They have music and dancing programs, as well as a full computer lab which is used by all age groups.

We visited the nursery for children aged two to four, which is on a separate property down the road. That is where Larissa spends most of her time. We also saw the church, who have set up a little shop to raise money for a missionary to go to Senegal, in Africa. *I love that*!! With all the poverty in Brazil, these people aren't wallowing in it and feeling sorry for themselves–they're looking to other countries where people might not know Jesus and sending people there. Magnificent!

A definite highlight was getting out the *footy*! I gathered up some of the teenage boys (and one brave girl) and explained to them how to kick and handball. They had a very limited space in which to play, so we had a bit of kick-to-kick.

At first they were all just standing around taking turns to get the ball, but then I explained that football is a contact sport and you can compete to get the ball–no pushing in the back or tackling when they don't have the ball. Well, you should have seen them–they loved it! It was great to watch the oval ball being enjoyed in a soccer-mad country.

On this day I had my own personal photographer–his name is Wesley and he's also a drummer. He came everywhere with us during the day and was snapping away. I made sure to ask if I could have a copy of the photos before I left Brazil. I asked about him toward the end of the day and found out that he's part of the government youth program that meets at the Project. He asked if he could be involved in media. So anything to do with websites, photos, music–that's what Wesley does.

The teenagers of the Project were busy on this day because they were preparing for a community party to be held in the evening. I was impressed to learn they had organized everything, which shows me that Compassion is doing a fantastic job of instilling a sense of responsibility, ownership and pride in their achievements into these amazing kids, which they probably wouldn't get at home or maybe even school.

Lunch was delicious, as it was at each Project. Their hospitality and generosity was incredible and humbling. The winner of the most interesting dish of the week goes to this Project. The mother of one of the Project kids made this: banana, wrapped in ham and cheese, cooked in the oven for 20 minutes. It was surprisingly nice. I think I must have been so baffled that I went back for seconds. It's just a combination that I never even imagined existing.

The faith that I witnessed from the people in this place was like nothing I've ever experienced before. It was defiant in the face of their circumstances. It was like the faith that knocked over the walls of Jericho. That enabled a shepherd boy to slay a giant. That Jesus says will 'move mountains.' I learned from the people of BR-329 that *we cannot limit God*. We can trust Him and believe for the seemingly impossible because the God we worship holds the *Universe* in His hand. He is a big, mighty, magnificent God.

One thing I love about Compassion is that it gives the children the freedom to dream about their future, without it being pie-in-the-sky wishful thinking. Because of the assistance and training the children receive from the church and Compassion, they have a very good opportunity to achieve their dreams.

BR-329 Home visits – Monalisa, Alynne and Larissa
When I visited, Larissa was four years old. She lives with her mum, grandma, two older brothers Rafael and Felipe, and baby sister Natalia. They had just moved house because mum got a job, so the grandma

was able to look after baby. The family was very blessed in this regard, because not everyone has a parent who is either able or willing to look after the grandchildren. Both brothers are sponsored by the same person from the United States. Judging by when Larissa was playing with the footy at the Project, she will have good ball skills when she gets older.

Alynne was 17 and in 10ᵗʰ grade. She has had four sponsors through her life and wants to be a lawyer. Alynne lives with her younger sister Gabriela, her mother, her 'aunt' (who is really just a close friend) and her aunt's daughter. She left the Compassion program because she got a job at a grocery store and her mother got a job too. They just moved house, and their circumstances improved to the point where they don't need the extra assistance. When she was growing up, Alynne missed two years of school resulting from family instability and moving around a lot. Fortunately she was still was able to go to the Compassion Project during this time. She is involved in church. Her mother would like to but is often busy and tired. Sometimes the aunt (lovingly) tries to drag the mother up and make her go because she thinks she's being lazy.

Monalisa was 18 and is now graduated from the Compassion program. She lives with her mother and younger sister Bianca. They live in a kind of apartment complex with three other families, some of whom are relatives. She has been described to me as an entrepreneur and dreams of being a vet. She had been recently offered three different government jobs and chose to work at a health insurance company. This was a blessing because when she broke her leg she was able to get health insurance to pay for it! I was Monalisa's second sponsor, so it's good that she's had the stability of a long-term sponsor. *She applied for a position in Compassion's Leadership Development Program in 2013 but was unsuccessful.*

Many of the home visits I've done have been filled with silence and awkwardness, but visiting Monalisa was completely different. Despite the language barrier, the conversation flowed freely and easily, we were comfortable with each other, and I appreciated their honesty in sharing their lives with me. I was blessed to play a part in the life of this beautiful young woman, however brief, and I'm sure God has great plans for her future.

Like with the other kids, I gave these three girls some gifts. Before I gave her the soft toy lamb I said to Monalisa "*I know you're 18, but I'm sure everyone loves a soft toy!*" I also gave them a necklace. Siblings received a clip-on koala and a postcard of Melbourne or Australian animals. The family received an Australia-themed clock and a small Australian flag. Monalisa and Alynne also received a scientific calculator courtesy of my friend Steve Jensen.

Birthday in Brazil!
Monday 1 October 2012

This was meant to be the day of all days–nine months in the making, the day where God's extravagant love would be demonstrated through a lavish act of generosity–me taking my ten Brazilian Compassion kids and their families to a special Park with a mini-zoo, horses, a pool and a soccer field and having a day we'd never forget.

In all honesty the day actually got off to a pretty crummy start for me. Firstly I woke up with a bit of stomach pain, which for me is never a good sign. Then, since I was paying for the day, my translator and I had to get to a bank. Simple enough? Yes, but it turned out that none of the machines accepted my bank's 'all-around-the-world' travel money card.

On the other hand, I learned later that the buses were due to pick the families up at 8.00am and everyone was there by 7.30, ready and raring to go! Bless them.

We ended up driving around Fortaleza for about 40 minutes which caused us to be late and really steamed me up. It affected me for probably the first 20 minutes of our day. Isabela hatched a plan to go to a local bank and withdraw the money from a teller which made sense, but it meant I would be without a translator for a while. I probably didn't think about it too much or it would have terrified me–a park full of Portuguese-speaking Brazilians.....and me!

So I spent the first twenty minutes of the day subdued and annoyed about the money thing. Most of the kids and siblings were aged under 12 so they headed straight for the pool and had a blast. I joined them but I didn't plan on going in. What could I do in a pool where the water was only thigh-high? Besides, I didn't bring a towel.

It turned out that both those excuses were lame, as I witnessed the pure, unrestrained joy of these kids laughing, splashing, playing and just being kids. I don't think I can underestimate the significance of this part of the day. Even though I visited some of their houses, I definitely didn't get a full picture of the difficulties they face in their lives, and here I was able to give them a rare opportunity just to have fun being kids.

I ended up 'getting over myself' and getting in with them, forgetting about the adult concerns of money and punctuality. I played ball, crawled around the pool on my hands and knees carrying five or six kids on my back, we played thumb-wars, paper-scissors-rock, sang silly songs and just had fun. I needn't have worried about a towel–I was dry after ten minutes in that sun!

The hardest part of the day was when Isabela left, and this coincided with lunchtime. The families were seated in their Project groups and didn't seem to mingle much. With no translator, I was unable to really interact with anyone.

Finally she returned and I went with some of the kids to look at the animals. There were various species of snakes, owls, other birds and monkeys. Peacocks and iguanas roamed around. The kids had a horse ride where they were led around by a Park worker. Some of the boys and Alynne came and had a kick of the footy with me.

I was happy with my ability to get around to everyone on the day. I made a special effort to have a couple of extended conversations with poor Monalisa, who was stuck in a wheelchair because of her broken leg. She generally stayed under the covered area where we had lunch. It was pleasing to see Jessica and Cristina open up to me more today, since at the Project on Thursday they had been shy and reserved the whole day. I still didn't get to talk to Cristina like I wanted to, but Victor assured me that after my visit she was talking about me and asking questions. I think some of them found it too difficult trying to communicate using a translator.

The biggest surprise came when we gathered for afternoon snack. On the way there I heard 'Happy Birthday' being played – by live music! My jaw dropped as I saw my new favorite band–the teenagers from BR-329 I met on Saturday! They had brought all their instruments and gear to the Park to surprise me. I was speechless and humbled at the effort they had put in to be there. They played a couple of tunes, then it was gift-giving time.

BR-329 gave me a CD with all the photos from my visit on Saturday as well as a drink bottle and t-shirt with a picture of me with Monalisa, Larissa and Alynne. BR-110 gave me a wooden 'Fortaleza' photo frame. Alynne gave me a pendant with an electric guitar on the end. Larissa gave me a bass guitar made of hardened clay that she had painted. Monalisa's mother gave me an embroidered table cloth-type thing with a picture and some writing on it. I asked her how long it took, thinking a long time. She shrugged and said "*An hour.*" Wow, okay then.

We prayed, then I jumped on the drums to play a couple of songs with my favorite crew. What impressed me most about them was the fact that in between songs half the group switched instruments and it still sounded just as good. They were very versatile. I had some spare clip-on koalas and it was a joy to be able to give one to each of the band members.

Then it was time for cake and winding down. We had some group photos. I got photos of the kids from each Project, then with their siblings, then with siblings, parents and Project workers. Finally one with all ten kids, and then the whole crew! There would have been about 30 family members altogether because many of the parents had to work. All ten kids had at least one family member with them.

Goodbyes were sad but not overwhelming. Some of the things that were said were very humbling to me. Larissa's mother said some nice things. In some ways the impact of my visit to Larissa could be considered negligible. She really didn't take to me at all, she was just too young. However, on the other hand I played a lot with her brothers on the

Fun Day and went goo-goo at her baby sister every chance I got. This
obviously had a positive effect on her mother. She was very grateful and
thankful for my visit and for the sponsorship. I rest in the hope that
visiting Larissa this young may plant a seed of value in her heart and she
can grow up knowing that I care about her because I've been to visit her
and God cares for her too.

I said goodbye to each of the band members individually. I was so proud
to know them and also humbled at their response to me. I can honestly
say that I've never had an effect like that on a group of teenagers. They
were so thankful for my visit but I was the one who was inspired by
them! And with that, the big adventure that was nine-months-in-the-
making was over.

The main lesson I learned from my time in Brazil is *'Don't Limit God.'*
When sharing about BR-329 New Life Project, I describe it as a little
bit of heaven. They serve 680 kids, many of whom live and work in
unimaginable circumstances. Yet this is what I witnessed when I was
there, from both kids and workers:

> *Life. Energy. Joy. Hope. Freedom. Peace. Achievement. Music.
> Dancing.*

These are things which cannot be acted or manufactured. They were
real, pure and genuine. I am convinced that the reason all these things
were present at BR-329 was because these people did not limit God and
what He could achieve through them. They did not put Him in a box
or put a roof over Him. Their dreams and vision for that Project and
community were huge and inspiring, despite the reality of the poverty
outside the walls. This included a two-storey building project that was
in progress and it was because of their faith and the belief that they are
doing God's work.

I can't help but compare this to the dreams and visions of most people
in the developed world. The aspirations of the people with the most
education and resources seem to revolve around either being famous

(whether for positive or negative reasons) or owning the latest/greatest/biggest/best (insert fleeting material possession here).

Why? Why make your dreams and visions all about yourself? We have one chance to make a difference to the world around us, and the best way to do that is to invest in other people.

As I mentioned, on the day I visited BR-329 the teenagers were running around busily preparing for a community party that they had organized and planned entirely themselves. This was incredible to me. Instead of running around the streets doing whatever teenagers in Brazil get up to, they were running a community party.

Compassion is instilling in these teenagers a sense of responsibility and pride in their achievements. It is silencing the voice of poverty which says to them *"You are useless and good for nothing. You will never amount to anything."* If what I saw in that place is anything to go by, the future of this community in Brazil is in good hands.

I couldn't help but recall 1 Corinthians 1:26-28: *"Remember, dear brothers and sisters, that few of you were wise in the world's eyes or powerful or wealthy when God called you. Instead, God deliberately chose things the world considers foolish in order to shame those who think they are wise. And he chose things that are powerless to shame those who are powerful. God chose things despised by the world, things counted as nothing at all, and used them to bring to nothing what the world considers important."*

Something I continually learn in my unusual lifestyle choice of sponsoring and advocating for so many kids is this: *If we want to make a lasting impact on other people's lives, all we have to do is step out, and God will use us. He uses the 'foolish, small and powerless' (people who come in humility) to shame the wise and achieve far greater things than if we are out on our own, in our own strength.*

Brazil Journey #2–September/October 2013

My visit to Brazil in 2012 impacted me so much I knew I had to go back again, although I didn't organize it nine months in advance this time. So I planned another trip for the school holidays of September/October and decided to have my birthday at Project BR-329.

Visiting Jasmiel at BR-453 Projeto Nova Vida (New Life Project)
Friday 27 September 2013

I love how when a person is a recipient of acts of generosity and kindness, it multiplies and inspires them to do the same. Kind of like the 'pay it forward' concept.

As I've already shared, back in 2011 I received a letter saying that the uncle of my Brazilian sponsored child Ana Cristina had been killed and the family had to move away. Two weeks later I received an email from Hayley Hughes, a Compassion employee who had visited Ana Cristina's Project. She took a photo of Ana Cristina holding one of my letters and sent me many pictures and videos of the day.

This act blessed my heart so much and it has been my privilege since then to give similar experiences to other sponsors when I have either met their child or given them gifts that the sponsor passed on.

In El Salvador I took a video of Loida and passed it onto her sponsor Lindsey. In Brazil in 2012 I took gifts for Erica from her sponsor Jennifer as well as a video and some photos. In Brazil in 2013 I took gifts from four different sponsors to pass on to their children.

Friday September 27 was my first day in Brazil and I was visiting a sponsored child that wasn't even mine. In early 2013, fellow Australian sponsor Brian Crawford posted a letter from his sponsored child Jasmiel on Facebook. It was incredibly impacting, as the kid was having a difficult time, and showed just what a difference a sponsor makes in the lives of the children and families.

I contacted Brian to find out what part of Brazil Jasmiel was from and he said Fortaleza, which is the same city that my seven kids were from. I offered to visit Jasmiel on behalf of the Crawford family, and that's where I found myself on this day. Brian and his wife Lisa have two kids–one with Cerebral Palsy and also a newborn, so it was a privilege and an honor to visit their boy on their behalf. God was once again using me to bless others.

Jasmiel lives in the small town of Pavuna and his mother recently left the family. This has led to all sorts of behavioral problems and presents a challenge for the Compassion staff who are caring for him. Jasmiel's father is unemployed at the moment and has three kids (Jasmiel has an older sister and a younger sister) to care for. All three kids in the family are sponsored which, in their situation, is literally the difference between life and death.

There were no Project activities on this day since it was a planning day, but that didn't matter one bit. Jasmiel was joined by his two sisters, Vitoria and Daniela, as well as two or three other friends, and we had a great morning playing soccer (with the ball his sponsors had given him), Australian football, table soccer, table tennis and jumping on the trampoline. This was the first Project I've been to that had a trampoline. I had a go but didn't last long–my knees don't like it when I jump.

I was blessed by the Project staff, so caring, friendly and enthusiastic. At each Project I have visited I love it how God has set it up so that the Compassion kids, who are the neediest in the community, are surrounded by such love and care. They literally experience the love of God through these wonderful adults and it often transforms their lives. I say 'often' because as the kids grow up they still have choices to make about which direction to take their lives, and unfortunately the right choices aren't always made.

We took a tour of the Project. The environment was colorful and child-friendly. I learned that the Project has been operating for five years and has increased from 100 to 305 kids. We then had a delicious filling lunch and there was no more trampoline for me after this.

Next we had a little devotion time where the kids sang a couple of songs and wonderful staff member Rosinha said some encouraging things. I was humbled to be the first sponsor to visit the Project and Rosinha said that when they found out I was coming, the staff were more excited than Jasmiel was!

Sponsor visits mean so much to the Compassion Project workers. They do an incredible job, literally giving their lives to be the hands and feet of Jesus to these kids and their families. I made sure to encourage them before I left, telling them that there are people thinking of them and praying for them. They are not forgotten.

Finally we visited Jasmiel's home. The house belonged to Jasmiel's grandparents and was passed on to his father, so that at least provides them with some stability. It is basically a brick box with some holes in the roof. It has a living area and one bedroom. I was told that Jasmiel and his father sleep on the bed while his sisters sleep on the floor in the main, narrow living area which has a rough dirt floor. I can't recall whether they have any sort of mattress. There was a small stove with some kitchen utensils. Three little kittens wandered around the place (and got stepped on at one point) and there were a couple of chickens and a rooster in the backyard.

One thing I was so encouraged to see was that Jasmiel's father clearly loves his kids deeply. He was pleasant to talk to and joined in our games of football and soccer. In the developing world, when a family breaks up it is usually the father that leaves, so I was witnessing a rare thing. I can only imagine his frustration at not being able to personally provide for his family but he is a godly man who hopes in God and is so thankful for Compassion and the Crawford family being there to support him and his kids.

Re-visiting BR-110
Monday 30 September 2013

After visiting Jasmiel, the next day I returned to BR-110. I was re-visiting my girls from Project BR-110, Pamella, Alice and Ana Alice. Taina left the Compassion program during the year because her family's financial situation had improved. This time there were Project activities going on and I was greeted by 60 wide-eyed and curious kids. They put on a bit of a show, but this was the highlight: in one of my letters I had mentioned that I love the song 'Alive' by Natalie Grant. One of the Project workers had worked on a dance with the girls, and they performed it, using the song. It's enough to make your eyes slightly damp. Playtime followed with singing and footy, they put on a delicious lunch and I was able to visit all three homes.

Birthday in Brazil 2013-A Day Like No Other
Tuesday 1 October 2013

The Bible says that if you give to the poor you are giving to God, and He will repay you. It's what I've made my life's mission to do and on this day I was repaid a million times over. I celebrated my 32nd birthday in Brazil at Project BR329. It is an incredible place where the presence of God is tangible and their faith is magnificent. It was a day of deep, pure and glorious joy, and we were drenched in God's love, mercy and grace which was expressed through generosity and selfless hospitality.

When I visited BR-329 (New Life Student Center) in 2012 I actually wondered how it would go, because I had only been sponsoring the kids there for about three months and we hadn't yet exchanged letters.

It was an incredible day. Their faith and generosity was astounding and the presence of God was thick in the atmosphere of the place. I had never felt anything like it. In addition they had an amazing 15-piece band of talented teenagers waiting to play for me and I was able to join them on the drums.

I knew I had to come back. So when I confirmed my plan to come back and celebrate my birthday in Brazil again, I knew BR-329 was the place to do it.

It was the second last day of the trip. I had been to Colombia, Ecuador and Peru and spent five days already in Brazil, so I was running purely on 'God-energy.' Of course I had my expectations of what the day was going to be like, but the actual day blew those expectations out of the water.

On a beautiful stinking hot day I was joined by Pamella, Ana Alice and Alice from BR-110; Christian, Jessica and Ana Cristina from BR-458 and Larissa from BR-329. Also making an appearance were Monalisa and Alynne, the two girls from BR-329 who graduated at the end of 2012, and Jasmiel, who I visited on behalf of a fellow sponsor.

The teenage band from 2012 was there ready to rock, with an extra drum kit just for me. We belted out some tunes and I did pretty well considering I hadn't played all year.

After this it was time to go upstairs with my kids and their Project workers and attempt to have something resembling a conversation. Conversation for me is hard at the best of times but when you have ten shy kids who speak another language, the degree of difficulty goes up a couple of notches. This was hard work and a challenge but I dug deep to find the open-ended questioning skills I've developed as a teacher and we managed to get them talking. We were able to talk a lot about our time together last year and what they had been doing since then.

I just spent some time soaking up the fact that we were all in the same room together. Talking didn't matter. Compassion sponsorship is about relationship and I was there with them.

BR-329 is a massive urban Project close to Fortaleza that now serves over 1000 children and teens. They host a successful government program that aims to help teens and young adults find their first job. Many of the churches aligned with Compassion realize that partnering with other organizations is a good strategy for building relationships, rather than remaining insular and isolated.

The number of children attending the Project is greater than the space they have, so last year they were undertaking a building expansion project, completely on their faith and trust in God to provide for them. I was amazed to see the progress made during this year. While it is not complete, they still use some of the unfinished rooms simply out of necessity.

We visited some of the classrooms in action. I could not believe they still had normal classes happening even with all the noise and excitement going on outside! Some of the children, who I did not know and had only just met, gave me little handwritten gifts. Pure love. One girl prayed for me and asked if she could lay her hand on my head while she did so. I had no words for that.

We enjoyed a lunch filled with traditional Brazilian yumminess, including a dish that I had been intrigued by last time I was here: fried banana, wrapped in ham and cheese. I normally don't have an adventurous palate but the verdict was: delish!

After lunch it was playtime. Footy, jumping castle, trampoline, fairy floss. Everything a good birthday party should have. It was a challenge spreading myself around to see everyone but I was able to have good conversations with some of the parents and Project workers. I was so pleased to see the way my kids interacted with each other, united by the blessing of sponsorship.

My youngest sponsored child is Larissa, who just turned five. When I visited last year she wouldn't have a bar of me. Not even a teddy bear could win me any points. I was relieved and thankful to see the difference that one year made. She was still shy but was a lot more responsive to me this time.

After a while of free play some of the kids performed a dance including Larissa up the front, always a couple of steps behind the others but very cute. Gifts were given, songs were sung, English was very bravely attempted to be spoken.

Then it was time for another surprise. All the kids went 'secretly' upstairs while I waited to be summoned. The time came, I opened the door and they exploded with....well I'm not exactly sure what was said, just lots of joyous noise and jumping up and down. There were balloons, party hats, crazy glasses with guitars on them, and a very musical cake. It was my third cake in four days and there would be another one at Project BR-458 the next day.

It was time for my speech. I'm no shrinking violet when it comes to talking in front of people so I started with this story:

I planned this trip back in June. I was so excited about coming back to Brazil that sometimes, when walking down the street, I would think of Brazil and just start smiling to myself, maybe even let out a little chuckle. The people walking or driving the other way would look at me thinking "What's up with that guy? What a weirdo, smiling and laughing to himself."

I thanked everyone for coming and celebrating God's goodness with me on this day, in particular my two graduates Monalisa and Alynne who chose to come back to see me even though they may have had work commitments or other things to do. It meant more to me than they knew.

I told them that I had shared the story of my previous visit to BR-329 with many people and kids had been sponsored because of it. I encouraged them to keep going, keep trusting in God to provide their needs and that they inspired me.

I told the kids that as much as I love them (and it's pretty clear I do), God loves them *so* much more. He has given me but a tiny glimpse of His love for them. He created them, He knows them and He has a plan for their lives, even if this may be hard to see sometimes.

As we ate cake and drank very-grapey grape juice I sat back, looked around at the room full of people that God had used me to impact in some way (and who had definitely impacted me) and I said "*Thanks.*" When you're blessed like I am it pretty much covers it, and there's not much else you can say.

This day truly was an ultimate gift of God – His grace, mercy and love poured out on all of us. To me it was a tiny taste of heaven and it will be hard to beat.

Re-visiting BR-458 (Projeto Sementinhas)
Wednesday 2 October 2013
On Wednesday, the final day of my trip, I revisited Project BR-458 where I sponsor Jessica, Christian and Ana Cristina. I knew it would be a hard day. I did my best to prepare myself for what I would see and experience but it was far harder than I even imagined.

Ana Cristina was my first sponsored child from Brazil. She is one of six kids and her mother was 13 when she had her oldest son. The family has endured a couple of shocking years involving drugs, murder and revenge killings, resulting in them being on the run. If it wasn't for a wonderful Project worker called Victor, who went and picked Ana Cristina up when she lived far from the Project, we would no longer be connected.

When I visited in 2012 I did not get to visit her home or family. I did not receive a letter from Ana Cristina this year and I made a special request on this trip to visit the home and meet her parents. I have visited 31 of my sponsored children in 12 countries and have seen some things that have wrecked my heart and spirit. Real life. Investing myself in these families so much comes at a cost, but I know it's what God wants me to do. It's slowly shaping the person He wants me to become.

So we headed out to Projeto Sementinhas (Little Seeds Project). There was small group of maybe 15 kids there at the time but none of my three. So I introduced myself, taught them about Australia, we sang songs and played games. I also got the footy out but with this group the soccer ball won the day, so we played some soccer. They didn't have an outdoor play area at the Project, but Pastor Josue lives across the road, so they go round to his backyard to burn off their energy.

I often get asked by the kids if I know how to play soccer and I always reply that I am a defender: I can get the ball off someone but once I have the ball I'm not very good. So I stayed in goals. It didn't matter that these kids were only ten years old. They were Brazilian and I was determined to beat them! I basically covered the small kid-sized goals and only conceded one.

Pretty soon we were quite tired because it was a very warm day so we went back to the Project. One thing I was looking forward to seeing was the church. When I visited last year it was being rebuilt. It had three walls, no roof and was basically a construction zone. The progress they made in one year was magnificent and it was all from the tithes and offerings of the church people. God has a habit of taking 'five loaves and two fish' (i.e. not very much) and turning it into food for thousands. He's good like that.

Then it was time to visit Ana Cristina. It's fair to say I was apprehensive. I breathed a prayer and away we went. To get there we walked down a narrow rocky path next to a stream of sewage. I tried to imagine living here with no other options or no way out. We came to her house, which was very well secured, and met her parents and some other relatives. I was greeted quietly and cautiously. I have detailed more about my visit with Cristina at the start of this book.

The more I heard of this family's situation, the more I wished I hadn't asked. On the surface it was an utterly hopeless tale. The extent of their dreams for their children are to be able to move to live in a different, safer area. This was survival and existence at its most raw. I was staggered and stunned at what I was hearing, yet I was still on my feet. Right now there was no happy ending with a bow and a cherry on top.

Unfortunately there is no quick fix for poverty; no miracle cure. Even as much as I love Compassion, I have never said that it's an instant solution to all life's problems. The Project workers come alongside the family and offer support for the children and their parents as best they can. It's a long term process.

This was the reality for my precious Ana Cristina. And yet, when I asked her what she was worried about or afraid of, she shrugged and said "*nothing.*" I got the sense that she has a quiet confidence in the protection of her parents, despite their inability to provide materially for her, and also in the Compassion staff. She has been shown enough love over her time at the Project to be secure in the fact that God loves her, no matter what else happens in her life.

I gave some gifts which were received with quiet gratitude. I thanked Mama and Papa for their honesty and trust in sharing their lives with me, and I left Ana Cristina with these words: "*As much as I love you, God loves you SO much more. He created you the way you are. Please always trust Him to protect you and provide for your needs.*" I was then able to pray for the family, first and foremost for provision of jobs, protection and safety.

As we walked back up the rocky path past the sewage stream, a thousand things were going through my head and yet I was composed. Halfway through lunch, the reality and the tragedy of what I just witnessed hit me hard, like a hammer to the gut over and over again. I excused myself, walked outside and cried out to God. I can't even remember what was said but I was just shell-shocked. I begged and pleaded for Him to intercede on behalf of that family and my precious girl. God had to remind me of my own words to Ana Cristina: "*They're mine. I love them so much more than you do. Trust me.*"

After lunch we went to visit Jessica. She has a mum, an older sister and a baby brother. The conversation was pleasant and once again we were joined by a bunch of assorted relatives. Jessica's mum is able to work from home, making and selling clothing. Jessica is a happy girl with a beautiful smile, but she is also very shy and basically spoke when she was spoken to. We managed to drag a half-decent conversation out of her. Out of all the gifts, she was quite taken by the 'Where's Wally?' book and wanted to start finding things in the book straight away.

Christian is my third sponsored child from BR-458 and unfortunately we were unable to visit his house on this day. I learned that his stepfather had decided to rough up his mother and did some damage, so his mum was embarrassed or ashamed to have visitors in the house. Christian is a bright young fella who *loves* his Bible. He said he has three of them in his house! I also brought him his own soft Australian football to keep.

After visiting Jessica we went back to the Project where we met the afternoon group of children. The procedure was basically the same. Introduce myself, sing songs, play games, kids laugh at me, then eat. Then it was time to go.

An interesting aspect of this day was my driver. Compassion had hired an eight-seater taxi for the day and the driver was an animated older gent who spoke a bit of English. My translator Anderson started explaining to him about Compassion and he was very interested. It turned out this was his second job driving on a sponsor visit and a Project Facilitator goes to his church. I loved his enthusiasm. He was joining in the songs, interacting with the kids and he even said later he was impacted by the emotion of the visit to Ana Cristina's house. It looks like Compassion has another advocate.

I strove to come up with a snappy, eloquent conclusion that would brilliantly sum up the complexity of all I witnessed on this day but I was unable to, so I'll settle with this:

> *I know I'm like a broken record, but today only confirmed to me the vital role that Compassion, the church and sponsors play in the lives of children and families in poverty. We are literally the difference between life and death. Apart from receiving food, clean water, medical assistance and education help, the children also receive Life and Hope for both this life and the next through the love of a sponsor and the opportunity to have a relationship with God the Creator of the universe.*

The House of God in Brazil-Faith That Moves Mountains

During my trip to Brazil in September 2013 I had the privilege of attending a church service. I wonder how many of us from the developed world consider going to church to be a privilege. Or is it just something we do, or take for granted?

The church is called *Assembleia de Deus Planalto Aeroporto*, in Fortaleza. It is open-air, with only a roof over the top and no walls. The reason I say it was a privilege was because, just like I felt in Mexico, I knew I was in the presence of spiritual giants. Their faith humbled and inspired me.

I spent a bit of time in the neighborhood over the previous few days during my time with my wonderful host and new friend, former Compassion sponsored child Debora Silva. The walk from the church to her house was a real eye-opener and an education for this sheltered little white guy. Drugs, violence, danger and abuse are prevalent. Debora's brother and sister had both seen a guy murdered near their house the previous night. You cannot sense much hope. The people of the church are courageous and they are warriors.

There is a battle going on in this world. It is not for oil, nuclear weapons or power, but for the soul of every human being. In so many places, on the surface evil appears to be winning, snatching away hopes, dreams and lives. But in my experiences, with the partnership of the church and Compassion, God is working through people who are committed to Him to bring His kingdom to earth.

These people are in the middle of this battle that is claiming lives and souls every day, yet they're standing in the presence of God and worshipping with such fervency and passion. It was profound and joyful.

Faith in God in the middle of such circumstances seems so crazy and counter-intuitive. But it's in the middle of these circumstances, when people realize that without God they have nothing, and cry out to Him, that he does His most powerful work, transforming lives and communities.

83

During this past week the church held a week-long seminar on the subject of 'Families'. One way Satan gets a foothold in the lives of people, particularly in children and teenagers is through the breakdown and disintegration of the family unit. Guilt, shame and anger can very easily take over. It is a major problem in this community. Debora told me that most of the children in the church are without at least one parent.

The church is fighting for the family, to set an example for the community about the difference that healthy relationships can make, with God's help.

I want to dedicate to these wonderful people this verse from the Word of God:

> *So don't get tired of doing what is good. Don't get discouraged and give up, for we will reap a harvest of blessing at the appropriate time* (Galatians 6:9).

So Many Open Doors-Sharing Jesus With the Kids of Brazil

One thing I love about being a servant of God is that it doesn't matter who you are, if you make yourself available and are willing, He will use you to do amazing things for the good of His kingdom. I am proof of that.

When I think about where I have come from to where I am now, I cannot help but drop to my knees in gratitude for God's goodness to me. In 1996 I was in 9th Grade. I was a friendless little runt, bullied and without purpose. That was my low point.

I grew up in a Christian home, yet did not fully commit to God until I was 21. Once I did that, God started to show me His purpose for me: Music, Teaching, Kids and Compassion. The journey with God and Compassion over the last seven years has been beyond my wildest dreams as I have submitted to God and am (hopefully) slowly growing to be more like Jesus.

With all the travelling I've done, there has been a fair bit of sacrifice involved on my part but I know that all I have is God's anyway, and nothing has been wasted. The main goal of my travels has been to visit the children I sponsor with Compassion International and their families, but what amazes me is the number of other doors God opened for me and the opportunities that have popped up to share His love with others. He has also used other people to bless me so much-hospitality, generosity, giving up their time to look after me, take me places and translate for me.

During my time in Brazil in September 2013, the Church I visited was running a week-long seminar on the topic of 'Families.' Wednesday night was Children's Night and the Pastor asked me if I would like to come and share something with the kids. I immediately said 'yes' but in truth felt so inadequate and wrong for the job. These kids were going through things in their young lives that were unimaginable to me, what could I possibly offer them?

Straight away I felt like God cleared His throat impatiently and was about to remind me of some home truths. This wasn't about me, or what I could do. "*Who are you sharing about?*" God asked me. "*Who are you representing?*" That's right, the Lord and Creator of the Universe. God had chosen me to bring His love to these kids and it wasn't about how I felt. He would give me the words and the strength.

Suitably chastised, I turned up on Wednesday night to a roomful of beautiful kids. The leaders up the front were talking and singing, and the kids seemed quite restless. As I watched them talking to each other and moving around, I wondered how they would respond to me. Even though I had Debora there to translate for me, would they stay engaged?

Well, I had nothing to worry about. As soon as I went up the front, the room went stone dead quiet, as they all stared at this weird-looking stranger with big ears, more hair on his face than his head, and speaking a language they didn't understand.

I shared with the kids the story of Jesus and Peter walking on the water. I told them that what I love about the Bible is that God has put the stories in there to teach us important things. We can learn something and get wisdom from all the stories in the Bible.

Using my best teacher-storybook voice I launched into a dramatic retelling of the story (well, as best I could considering I had only one microphone that I had to put in Debora's face after every sentence).

I shared with them that the storm in the story represented the bad things that sometimes happen in our lives, and that while Peter had his eyes on Jesus he was okay, he was walking on the water. But when Peter took his eyes off Jesus he began to sink, which represents the worry, fear and doubt we feel when bad things happen in our lives. I also shared that when Jesus rescued Peter, he didn't stop the storm straight away.

Some people believe that when we become a Christian, God will take all the bad stuff away and give us a perfect and happy life. That is completely untrue. Jesus says that "*in this world we will have trouble*" (John 16:33) but He will help us through the storm if we keep our eyes on Him and trust Him.

I also had a go at teaching them the song 'My God Is So Big' complete with actions, which was a bit of fun.

After the night finished, many of the children came up to me for a hug or to have a photo taken with me. Being able to bless them in this way was profound and amazing. Because I was friendly and engaging, many of them also tried to talk to me, not fully grasping that I didn't understand a word they were saying. I just had to keep pointing to Debora and saying "*talk to Debora*" and "*no fala Portuguese.*"

It was a privilege and an honor that God chose me to speak to these kids. It is heartbreaking and mind-blowing to imagine some of the things they have gone through and will go through in their lives and I can only hope that God will use the words I spoke on His behalf to plant a seed of faith and hope for their future.

Journey #3–South & Central America, January 2013

When I returned from my first Brazil trip in 2012, if I wasn't already a Compassion lunatic, I was now. I caught the travel bug in a big way. Most of my sponsored kids ended up being from South and Central America. There's no particular reason for this, it's just the way it worked out. So I planned a trip there for January 2013. This was not just any old trip, but it was highly ambitious and even crazy.

The numbers:
- 14 children visited
- 7 countries (Mexico, Guatemala, Nicaragua, El Salvador, Ecuador, Dominican Republic and Haiti)
- 3 weeks

The trip was a life-changer. I was in over my head, out of my depth and many other clichés. It literally took me months to process many of the situations and circumstances I witnessed and found out about. One of the meanings of compassion is 'to suffer with,' and that was certainly true of me during these three weeks. It wasn't made any easier by the fact that two days after I returned to Australia I started a new job teaching at a new school. I visited homes, schools, churches, Compassion Projects, Fun Parks, malls, restaurants and zoos.

What follows is the accounts of many of the visits I was blessed to experience on this trip, written just hours after they happened. *The details are real, raw and often confronting.* My heart was broken so many times, but each time it just confirmed to me more and more that Compassion is God's answer to fighting poverty and for these families He is their only hope.

Go into all the World

Visiting **Allison** in Mexico
Experiencing the House of God in Mexico
Visiting **Danna** in Mexico
Visiting **Olga** in Mexico
(*Wealth and Poverty Collide*)

Visiting **Josefa** in Guatemala
(*Waiting For Her Father to Change*)

Visiting **Yeymi** in Guatemala
(*Things Like This Don't Happen To Me Or People I Know*)

Visiting **Mayra** in Guatemala
(*Lessons Learned, Attitudes Adjusted*)

Re-Visiting **Rosa** in El Salvador
(*A Family Reunion*)

Visiting **Katherine** in El Salvador
(*Poverty of Family, Hope for the Future*)

Visiting **Jacqueline** in Ecuador
(*A Day of Pure Joy and Learning About Trust*)

Visiting **Antonio** in Nicaragua
(*The Turning Point*)

Visiting Allison, Danna and Olga in Mexico
Allison
Saturday 12 January 2013

After about four hours sleep in my hotel in Mexico City, I was up at 6am to get ready for the first visit day of what I called my 'Central America Mega-Tour' (even though Ecuador is South America and Dominican Republic and Haiti are in the Caribbean).

I met my translator/lifesaver Irma at 7.00am. She was with me for the entire four days in Mexico, for which I was grateful. She has been working for Compassion for 12 years. We jumped on a bus for an 80 minute trip to San Martin Texmelucan to meet Allison. At the bus station we were picked up by the Pastor who has been at his church for 17 years. Compassion Project ME785 has been operating for six years and has a couple hundred kids.

In my visiting experience so far I have found that many of the Pastors who have churches involved with Compassion have been there a long time. I was told that the city of San Martin Texmelucan has 130,000 residents, with only about 10,000 Christians, so they are the minority.

When we arrived at the Project, we walked in to a church full of kids of all ages. I did my best to introduce myself in Spanish (thanks to Microsoft Word translate tool) and sang them the song 'God of Wonders.' There was no guitar, so I had to struggle along on the piano–chords only! I asked if anyone had a sponsor from Australia and no hands went up. I found out from talking to some of the kids later that some of them don't even know which country their sponsor comes from, and even have trouble saying the name of their sponsor.

I then met Allison and her family–Mama, older sister Veronica and younger sister Alicia. Allison's Dad was at work. He makes clothes with a couple of his brothers and extended family, then they go off to sell them on weekends, so the kids don't see their dad much.

I joined some of the kids for a snack, and got to know the family better. The kids asked me questions about myself and Australia. I taught them a couple of fun camp songs, Thumb Wars (*1, 2, 3, 4 I declare a thumb war!*), then I got out the footy, although there wasn't much play space. ME785 is an urban project and there are currently massive building extensions happening in order to expand the Project. So their play space is a construction zone. Nevertheless, we made the best of what we had and I took a group of 25 kids out to have a go at handballing an Australian football. Interesting....

After a while we took a tour of the Project. I saw the classrooms, medical room, kitchen, office, and pretty soon it was evident why they need to make extensions–there's just no room! However, the staff do the best with what they've got and are being the hands and feet of Jesus to these kids. The kids at this Project were a happy, curious bunch and I felt very loved and accepted. I even had some kids wanting my autograph. Weird... I just wrote them a little message and signed off with a smiley face 'David from Australia.'

Meeting Allison was amazing. Having met so many of my sponsored kids, part of me was thinking *"Surely I'd be used to it by now? Surely I know what to expect? Surely it would lose a bit of the thrill, excitement and nerves?"* The answer to that is a resounding '*no*'! When you make the decision to invest in a little soul for both this life and eternity, supporting them with money, love, encouragement and letters, and you finally get to *be with* them and see what their life is like–where they live, where they play-not much else comes close to that feeling.

I had been sponsoring Allison for a year at this time. She is a super-sweet, affectionate 8-year-old. Her older sister Veronica is 10, and her younger sister Alicia is three. Mama is 27 and was very engaging and easy to talk to. She sells sandwiches and tortillas outside her daughter's school and takes the little one with her. Both Allison and Veronica are top of their classes at school. Veronica is also sponsored but her sponsor never or rarely writes. Not good enough in my book.

In May 2012, I received a letter saying Allison's Project was going to close at the start of 2013 and they weren't sure whether Allison would go to a new Project I was given the option to cease my financial sponsorship until the problem was sorted out, but I prayed about it and felt that with God's help I should continue to support Allison, despite the uncertainty of what lay ahead. I found out today that from June to September Allison did not attend her Project at all, even though it was still running. From hearing Mama talk about it I think this may be because they weren't happy with the decision to close the Project down. In October the girls started going to ME785.

We left the Project sooner than I would have liked because of the schedule. With the sponsor visits, as well as seeing the Project and the child's home, often we will go to a park/zoo/mall as a special treat. The problem with this is they are often far away from the child's town and much travelling is required. It's also usually just the child and one parent rather than the whole family. Whenever I visit, my personal priority is to visit the Project and the home, and spend as much time with the whole family as possible. Anything after that is a bonus.

So today we rushed off from the Project and took Allison's family to a place called 'Hacienda de Chautla' which is a historical castle and museum, and we got the guided tour. It was good and has a nice natural lake, but is not necessarily somewhere I'd take three kids under 10. However, Irma told me the girls enjoyed it and had been wanting to go there, so that's what matters I guess.

On the way out I asked the Pastor what sort of fish you can catch in the lake. He said there are two types, and when you catch a fish you pay a certain amount to take it with you. He also took this question to mean that I wanted to have a go. I tried so hard to refuse but before I knew it a rod was in my hand and my sponsored child and her family were all watching me. I never have been, nor ever will be a fishing person, for me, the only good thing to come from fishing is the classic Homer Simpson line "Na-na-na-na-na-na-na-na, fishing!" There are many things I'd rather do before I go fishing. So I duly stuffed up the cast (is that what it's called when you throw the line into the water?) by getting the line tangled, handed back the rod and stormed off in a huff. Well, not really, but my body language wasn't positive for a few seconds.

For lunch we went to a restaurant called 'Nila Restaurante', and this was the first time the girls had ever been out to eat. This made me feel quite privileged that I was able to give them this opportunity, and it's something we just take for granted. Allison is only 8 and her plate contained a couple of massive pieces of fish. I was quietly skeptical about whether her meal would get finished, but by golly she did it!

The last stop for the day was their family home. They live in a busy city street and it is part of a 'complex' of units that are hidden behind a high sheet metal fence. Their extended family lives in the same group of houses. We talked for a while, they showed me around the house, we looked at some of their family photos, they got out the letters I'd sent Allison and I gave them some gifts. For each child I visited on this trip I gave the following:
- a teddy bear, a 'Jesus' pendant and a bead necklace for the child (soccer ball for Antonio, my one boy on this trip);
- a clip-on koala and a postcard for the siblings;
- a koala snow globe and an Australian flag for the family.

I am always affected by the generosity and hospitality shown by the families on my sponsor visits. They may not have much, but what they do have they share willingly and graciously.

Experiencing the House of God in Mexico
The first stop on my visit to Jiquipilas, Mexico to visit 9-year-old Danna, was church. What better place to be on a Sunday morning!? We were picked up from Tuxtla, a two-hour drive away, by the Director of Project ME738. His name is Aurelio and he has been in the job for 10 years. Compassion doesn't normally host visits on Sundays but because of my schedule they were flexible and agreed to host me. This just meant I didn't get to see the Project in action but what I got instead was still incredibly memorable and impacting.

The Project ME738 is connected to 'The First Church of the Nazarene (Jesus).' Nazarene is a Pentecostal denomination in Mexico. Some of Danna's family go to the 'Second Church of the Nazarene' instead.

It was a warm day and the church was very open-no windows, and no enclosed wall on one side. I figured the weather must be warm/hot the whole year round but was surprised when the family said that this wasn't typical weather. I can't imagine what it's like when it's colder. Translator Irma and I arrived before church started and were escorted to the front row, where I met Danna. She was shy and polite. During the service she was busting to go out with the other kids but Mama made her stay in and sit next to me. I felt sorry for her.

The music was led by a team of six young guys and was phenomenal and passionate, which are two words that could be used to describe the whole service. It didn't matter that I didn't understand a word they were saying, apart from maybe "*Gracias Senor*" (thank you God) or "*Nombre de Jesus*" (name of Jesus). I did recognize the songs 'Open the Eyes of My Heart' and 'Agnus Dei.'

I felt the presence of God in that place. The lads displayed incredible talent and ability on their instruments, swapped instruments at times, and played without any sheet music. I learned they also sometimes travel around and lead worship at other churches in the area. I was thrilled to find out later that three of those guys were former Compassion-sponsored kids, now using their gifts and talents for the glory of God. I love stories like that!

On this day there were between 200 and 300 people at the church. It was interesting to observe the way they did things and how different it was to a lot of churches I've been part of. There was a genuine healthy fear of the Lord in the place and their faith and joy, even in their circumstances, was tangible. I was moved to tears and beyond words; grateful and humbled to be there, feeling like I was in the presence of true worshippers.

The Pastor of the church (who has since passed away) had been very sick and appeared quite old and frail. He made his return to church on this day. I only talked to him briefly but he clearly inspired the people of his church and had authority and their respect.

When the worship leader prayed, he or she got down on their knees. Postures of worship were very important–about three different times in the service, about 50 people or so came to the front and lay prostrate before God. The people were very physically affectionate with each other and with me. I was embraced more times than I could count, which is something I'm not used to but have become comfortable with.

A young woman preached on this day (for over an hour) and she was strong, bold and passionate. There were no notes or fandangled PowerPoint slides. The only tools she used were a whiteboard with three dot points and her sword–the Word of God.

A definite highlight was being able to get up and play the drums with the music team lads. It was a big ask for them but I asked if they knew the song 'One Way, Jesus', and sure enough they did, so we played it. At first the people were just sitting, treating it like an item, but one of the church leaders exhorted them to stand and soon we had a church full of 300 people celebrating Jesus as "*the Way, the Truth and the Life*".

As I was belting it out, a thought dawned on me that was so profound and humbling I nearly fell off my chair: *I'm doing what God has gifted me to do (playing drums), and we might come from 'different universes', but I'm leading a church of 300 Mexicans in joyfully celebrating and glorifying OUR God, the Creator of the universe.* It doesn't get much better than that.

After we finished playing I got off the drums but they called for an encore, so we played 'Trading My Sorrows', which they had sung earlier in the service. I was then able to share briefly with the people. In all honesty I felt so inadequate, small, empty and broken. I was coming from such a privileged and blessed country where we take *everything* for granted and have everything we could ever need or want, and I was standing before these spiritual giants who have nothing materially but are so content, joyful and filled with faith and trust in their loving God. What was I supposed to say?

Thankfully, God gave me words. This is what I shared *"I have only been in your community for a very short time and I can tell your lives are hard. I cannot pretend to know what your lives are like but need to tell you, I can feel your faith, joy and passion for Jesus. I can only encourage you, as the apostle Paul says in the Bible to "Fight the good fight, finish the race and claim the prize that Jesus has for us – eternal life." True hope, joy and freedom only come from faith in Jesus."*

Visiting Danna in Mexico
Sunday 13 January 2013
Danna's family consists of Mama, older sister Silvia, 10, and older brother Miguel, 14. Silvia is sponsored by a Korean family and has received a total of one letter and photo. Miguel was sponsored but left the program. I got the impression that, for whatever reason, he just didn't want to be part of it anymore. They have aunts and cousins living next door. Mama works at Casa Dias ('Day House'), a government organization where people get support and learn skills.

When I first saw their house I asked how many other people live with them, but it was just Mama and the three kids. I thought it was quite big for a family of four. They have electricity, a bathroom, one bedroom, and dirt floor. The house has wooden foundations and an iron sheet roof. What really struck me is how this family take pride in their home despite their humble circumstances. They still had their Christmas tree and decorations up, as well as a tribute in the corner to their deceased grandmother–a table with a photo, candles and a Bible.

The church service did not finish until after one o'clock so we shelved our original plans. We were going to take Danna to Tuxtla, which was a large city about 80km away, for lunch. However, whenever I visit my

Compassion kids my priority is spending as much time as I can with the family and seeing their home and environment. So someone went out and bought some lunch and we ate at Danna's home.

We were joined for lunch by the little cousins and a couple of aunts. There was good conversation and lots of questions. I was humbled by their generosity and hospitality. They did ask what I thought of their home and neighborhood but they didn't seem overly concerned, insecure or ashamed. Once again, there was a sense of contentment in what God has provided for them.

Danna's father has not been on the scene for eight years, since she was a baby. Mama said he left for the United States to look for a job and never came back. An all-too-common story in these parts of the world. I asked her if she was expecting that to happen when he left and she said "no", so it wasn't like they were fighting and he stormed out. I could feel a sense of loss there. This makes Miguel the man of the house and my role as Danna's sponsor even more significant.

After lunch our little tribe (seven kids, six adults) headed out into the neighborhood. It seemed quiet and safe with paved roads, and Danna said she enjoys living there. Our first stop was a public football stadium, complete with synthetic surface. I had already introduced them to the strange, red egg-shaped ball that is an Australian football so we were planning to have a kick. However, there were already a bunch of teenage boys at the park playing that *other* football, the round-ball variety.

They were on a break, since their soccer ball had burst and they were waiting for someone to bring back a replacement ball, so the kids and I got on and had a kick of the footy. I can't imagine what the soccer boys were thinking at this sight! I tried to get the lads involved by kicking it near them, but only had one or two takers. Most of them were bemused by it and treated it almost like a bomb when it came near. However, it didn't stop them wanting to have a photo with me when they found out I was Australian. There's now a bizarre photo of me among a bunch of Mexican soccer boys, wearing a New York Knicks shirt (American basketball), an Aussie cap and holding an Australian football!

After this we headed up the road to a local soccer ground and playground, where there was a proper match going on. Here I had an interesting bathroom experience. Being a local soccer match in Mexico, even the change rooms are guarded by an armed policeman and he led me into one of them, where there was a solitary toilet in the corner. When the time came to wash my hands I looked around puzzled for a sink, but he came and pointed to the cistern of the toilet, which was indeed filled with water but obviously not the kind I was originally thinking! So for the first time in my life I washed my hands in the cistern of a toilet...

The kids and I then had a play on the playground. I did not need my translator Irma for this because fun on a playground transcends every language. The equipment was rusted and quite primitive but they even had one of those 'wizzy-dizz' rides that you hop on and someone pushes it round until everyone gets dizzy. They're the ones that are very rare, if not extinct, in Australia because the local councils are too scared of getting sued if someone inevitably gets hurt on them.

We finally headed back to the house for gifts and goodbyes, sweaty and content after a couple of hours of simple fun. I much preferred this to the original arrangement, which would have had us doing a lot of sitting in cars.

A holy moment I have been able to experience in every visit is the giving of gifts. I brought pretty much the same thing for each child, with a couple of extra things for two girls having a birthday and the ones with larger families.

I gave every child a teddy bear, even the older ones. One cannot underestimate the comfort and security a person gets from having their own teddy bear, particularly considering the lives these kids have. My

one boy Antonio was given a soccer ball and the girls received simple silver necklaces with a fish symbol containing the word 'Jesus.'
After seeing the living conditions of pretty much all the kids I have visited, I was always struck by the symbolism as I put the necklace gently round each girl's neck and pointed out the word on the Fish - *Jesus*. He is their only hope, and I'm very blessed to know that the majority of my Compassion kids already recognize and acknowledge this.

Visiting Olga in Mexico – Worlds of Wealth and Poverty Collide
Tuesday 15 January 2013
Today was a day of heartache and incredible joy. Massive contrasts. The worlds of wealth and poverty did not just collide today, they exploded in my face, and my head and heart are confused. I'm not pretending that I'm the first person to struggle with this and I certainly won't be the last, but I'm no longer some idealist/bleeding-heart/do-gooder whose only knowledge of the inequality in the world is theoretical by nature.

By golly, it became real to me today.

I have been investing in Olga's life through Compassion sponsorship for two years. She is a tiny ten-year-old and is one of eight siblings aged 6 to 20. I only met two of them today because it was a normal school/work day. This meant there was no action at the Project either. We met at the Project, had a tour of the rooms and the church and I 'showed off' on the drums. We then had an incredibly moving time where several songs were exchanged. I sang to Olga, she sang to me and her father sang to me as well. Their gratitude for my support and for the impact that God and Compassion have had on their lives was heartfelt and genuine.

Olga has a mum and a dad who love their kids very much, but struggle to provide for them. I was not expecting to see that their house only had two and a half walls around it. The front wall is only partly completed and one of the sides of the house has wire fencing instead of a wall. It is basically made of sticks and they have one bedroom for ten people. They do not have access to running water in their house and bottled water is expensive. There are lots of chickens and dogs running around in the yard. Photos of me and my family were featured prominently outside the bedroom.

Olga's dad works as a motor-taxi driver and a fisherman and spends most of his income paying it off. He often gives free rides to the kids from the Compassion Project who cannot get there any other way. I know God will bless this selfless act. He very generously rode me, my translator Irma, Olga and his wife around the neighborhood and showed us the nearby beach. What a sight that must have been for the neighbors.

The parents show an incredible defiant faith in God that flies in the face of their circumstances, and their gratitude brought me to my knees. I met the oldest daughter, who is 20, and the second son, who is 16. The others were all at work or school. The older ones choose not to go to church and aren't Christians as far as I'm aware. I know Mama and Papa fervently pray for their kids and I know God hears them.

In complete contrast to what I had just witnessed of Olga's home life, in the afternoon we toddled off to a shopping mall in Tapachula, a large town about 30 minutes away. Just your everyday, standard mall in my part of the world. Having just visited the family's house and seen how they live (remember: two and a half walls), this was culture shock for me beyond anything I had experienced. It was Olga and Mama's first time at the mall. When we got there we hopped on one of those little trains that goes around the mall and toots people to get out of the way. It was funny seeing a young Mexican hombre greeting his mates with cool-dude high fives as he drove a little tooting train around.

The little train trip was a mixture of funny and sobering moments. It was an eye-opener, for me as well as Mama and Olga. I watched them take it all in and my heart broke. I struggled to reconcile the two worlds I had just been a part of, so close together. They were seeing people just like them, who lived only a short car ride away, but who may as well have been from another planet. I wondered what was going through

Mama's head as we travelled past Walmart, jewelry shops, shoe shops, food shops and others, selling everything imaginable in unimaginable quantities.

After having some Domino's pizza we went to Playland Circus, which is your everyday-average amusement game arcade. I have to admit I initially wondered about taking them to a place like this, as I consider them to be an over-priced frivolous waste of money. However, on this occasion I can say I was very, very wrong. I had a couple of *wins* today as a result of being a clueless gringo who had come all the way from Australia. One was that I got to join Olga on the massive bouncy castle. Initially she was the only one on, and you could sense her enthusiasm waning after about two minutes. My translator Irma managed to convince the guy to let me have a jump and the transformation in her demeanor was incredible.

I don't think sponsors can ever fully understand the impact that their visit has on the child, but I got a pretty good indication on this afternoon. I cannot adequately describe the pure excitement, joy and delight Olga displayed as we bounced, jumped, ran and slid for (what felt like) about 30 minutes and I certainly exhausted my aerobic capacity. That jumping castle was a 'Temple of Joy.' She even brought on the teddy bear I had given her as a gift and started throwing it around! A highlight for me was when we were attacking the inflatable punching bags that were part of the jumping castle, and each time I punched them I said "*punch, punch, punch.*" In her excitement, Olga tried to copy what I was saying but it came out as "*woosha-woosha-woosha.*"

We then played some of the other games. Olga was unrestrained in her glee as she shot basketballs in the hoop (very well, I might add!) and played air hockey. She even won enough tickets to get herself a prize, which I know is something she will always treasure. My earlier grumbles about the way I spend my money went out the window as it dawned on me what a rare and precious experience this was for both Olga and her mother. Absolute gold!

On the way to the airport, the one thing I could not get out of my head was the image of Mama looking around at the foreign world of the mall when we were riding the train. I tentatively asked the question, "*What were you thinking?*"

I was not expecting her answer.

"*I was very content because I had never been to the mall before, and I was happy because my daughter Olga was happy to be there too.*"

Well said, Mama.

Visiting Josefa, Yeymi and Mayra in Guatemala

Visiting Josefa in Guatemala–Waiting For Her Father to Change
Wednesday 16 January 2013

To get to 14-year-old Josefa's community required a three-hour trip, from Guatemala City to just outside Quetzaltenango, in the west of the country. The journey was an eye-opener and I drank everything in. We were deep in the mountains and passed a volcano or two. The beauty of the scenery was breathtaking, but I'm sure that it's little consolation to the hundreds of people we passed who were just aimlessly standing by the side of the road or eking out a measly existence selling random stuff at roadside stalls.

In Australia, when we see people walking or driving it's likely that they have a purpose in where they're going; that they have something important to do or somewhere important to be. That's not the sense I got on this trip. We were in the middle of nowhere, in the mountains of Guatemala, far from the nearest large town. It made me think about those people; the old man with a bunch of sticks on his back, the woman with a baby wheeling a bicycle. What were they doing? What did their day ahead look like and what did they see when they looked into their future?

We finally arrived at Josefa's community, which is Mayan, so the clothing was intricate, colorful and beautiful. I met Josefa and her family at the Compassion Project (Mama, Papa, two younger brothers Carlos and Mark, and two younger sisters Andrea and Melani) and they presented me with a traditional Guatemalan men's garment, which I put on to honor them despite the stifling humidity. I would also receive one the next day from Yeymi's family to add to my collection.

There was nothing happening at the Project because it was morning and the kids were at school. They would be back in the afternoon. We had a tour and I would say it was one of the least resourced Projects I have seen, which is an indication of the status of the community. There were leaks and the place wore the battle scars of earthquakes. However, I talked to some of the Project workers, saw the cupboards full of student records, immunizations etc. and I knew that God's love was in that place. They are doing the best they can with what they have.

While we were there, a parade went past. I was told the Catholics celebrate a different saint each year and this year the parade was in honor of 'The Black Christ', whatever that is. The dancers wore masks which were quite macabre and creepy. People are also into self-flagellation, crawling to the church on their hands and knees from a long way away. The music was funky though.

We took a walk to visit Josefa's extended family, down the main street of the neighborhood. We dodged the scary masked dancers, cars, trucks, bikes and buses, and on the way back school had just finished, so we passed hordes of kids looking at me strangely. This was because I was wearing the traditional Guatemalan garment that Josefa's family had presented me with and probably didn't look much like a Guatemalan. I met Josefa's grandparents, aunts and uncles and saw where they and her father eke out their income making and selling garments. Despite their circumstances they were quietly content and joyful, and welcomed me into their home.

We then went back to the family's house and had a tour. I presented gifts and taught them about Australian football. I kept asking Josefa about how she helps around the house. Does she help in the kitchen? Does she help look after her baby brother? The reply to both was *"A little bit, but I don't have time."* I was appalled to discover the reason for that: Josefa and 12-year-old Carlos both have to work 6 hours a day making men's shoes just to help the family and be able to afford to go to school, because of the lifestyle choice of her father.

Josefa dreams of being a doctor. When I was at the Project I saw Josefa's school results. She is in either 8th or 9th grade and her results are fairly average. I would 'bet the farm' that those poor results would have something to do with having to work 6am–12pm six days a week before going to school.

I just realized some people might be reading the accounts of my Compassion children's lives and be thinking *"Gee whiz, he's painting a pretty grim picture here. Where does this Compassion business fit in and how does it help them?"*

For all my advocacy with Compassion, I'm not for a moment pretending that it's a miraculous quick fix. Poverty is disgusting and is not easily solved. People also have choices to make. What Compassion does is come alongside the family and supports them, in a long-term strategy for the family to *lift themselves* out of poverty. Compassion assists with (they don't pay all) costs associated with the child and family's medical, educational, nutritional and spiritual well-being. It provides them with a sponsor in a far-away country to come alongside them and offer words of encouragement, hope and love.

For lunch I took the whole crew to Pollo Campero (chicken country) where you can 'Enjoy, Dream and Jump', and then we came back to the Project to meet the kids. We visited each classroom individually, I introduced myself and took questions from the kids. The reaction varied from class to class. Some were wide-eyed and silent, staring at this big, white, bald, smiley stranger speaking a weird language, holding a weird red egg-shaped ball and they didn't know what to think. Others were jumping out of their skin to ask questions and enjoyed having me in there. I made sure to encourage them that God loves them and I was happy they were there in the Project where they could feel safe and loved.

The goodbye was gut-wrenching. We were going to do it out on the street in front of all the Project kids but I wanted to do it privately just in case I cried, which I did. Josefa was incredibly affectionate. She was by my side the whole day and was distraught at the end. I spent five minutes just consoling her while she sobbed. That will never leave me. The older kids have a different sense of how significant a visit from their sponsor is. Praying with these families is a holy experience and the inadequacy that I feel is ever-present. But I was able to speak Words of Life over this precious family and leave them in His hands.

Visiting Yeymi in Guatemala
'This Doesn't Happen To Me or People I Know'
Thursday 17 January 2013
What I saw and heard today was surreal. I remember thinking repeatedly: *"This doesn't happen to me or people I know."* The details in this story are all real and true. They happened to me a matter of hours ago. I hope you are inspired, encouraged and challenged.

Sponsoring a child is a good thing. Today I found out that you can never underestimate the importance of a sponsor in a child's life, and that's the way God designed it. Often you don't find this out for real until you make the decision to go beyond the *'face on the fridge and monthly bill'* stage. When you start writing regular letters, the child trusts you more, gradually opens up and you find out more about their lives.

When you go even further and choose to enter their world by visiting their home, school and environment, all sorts of things can open up and be discovered and often it can get very messy. It is a scary but exhilarating place to be, and you realize that for all 'we' are doing as sponsors, the reality is that only God can bring them true freedom, hope and joy.

Today it got messy for me.

I visited 10-year-old Yeymi in Guatemala. I also met her three sisters Ella (15), Alessandra (13) and Tania (8). I have been investing in Yeymi's life for two years now. I was very happy to hear that all the other kids are jealous of her because of all the letters and pictures she gets. Not in a prideful way, of course. It just vindicates the efforts I make to write all my kids once a month because the letters are so important in encouraging the child that someone loves them and they are special and valued.

Another tiny tear to my heart came when Yeymi said that she considers me to be like her Papa. She does have a father but he's two-and-a-half hours away in Guatemala City during the week, working in 'construction' earning maybe 40 Quetzals ($5) a day.

During the visit to the house, which is owned by Yeymi's grandmother, I was given information that was like pieces of a disturbing jigsaw puzzle which I didn't put together until later. They have three rooms in their house which are used as bedrooms. They have some uncles that sleep in one room. All four sisters sleep in another room, in the one bed.

They have a third room which they call the 'guest room.' It is relatively well fitted out with a decent sized bed and mosquito net. I asked why a couple of the sisters didn't sleep in this room. All they replied was "*We are afraid of being alone.*" Yeymi also showed me boxes of clothes in this room that belong to each member of her family. I found out later that these are the only things the family owns – the clothes on their backs.

We met all sorts of aunts, uncles, cousins, grandparents (Yeymi's abuela is 55, but looks a lot older) as well as her great-grandparents who have been married 61 years and are still working, feeding and looking after 3000 chickens out of necessity.

Yeymi's Mama asked if we could give her a lift to Guatemala City when we left after lunch. I was puzzled and asked why. It turns out every two weeks she joins her husband when he goes off to work in Guatemala City for the week, and leaves her four daughters in the care of their grandmother. I didn't delve any further at that point and agreed to take her.

For lunch I took 11 family members from four generations to Pollo Campero, including the grandma and the great-grandmother. The only males in our group were me and a three-year-old cousin. I'm sure we would have looked quite the motley crew to the other restaurant patrons.

We said our goodbyes and my translator/lifesaver Mayra, Mama and I started our two-and-a-half hour journey to Guatemala City. We began in silence, and when I tentatively started our conversation I could not imagine where it would lead. This is what I found out.

Mama is about to turn 30 and her husband is 32. I was smack-bang in between them at 31, yet there could not be a greater chasm between our lives. They were married when she was 14 and he was 16. Mama was 15 when their oldest daughter was born. She did not finish school and has never worked. When she joins her husband every two weeks in Guatemala City, all they can afford to rent is a single room and she claims she does not work because "*I do not know my way around.*" From what Mama said, all she does is cook for him.

Meanwhile, four girls are without their Papa for five days of the week and without their Mama for every second week, being looked after by their grandmother with no male figure to protect them. I started joining dots but didn't want to jump to any conclusions. The comments about the uncles, me being like Yeymi's Papa and the girls being afraid of being alone were starting to make sense, and it left a bitter taste in my mouth.

However, worse was to come. Eight months ago the family was living in their own house and Mama was in the city with her husband. Her uncle, who is an alcoholic and a 'bad man', came into the family's house when no-one was there and stole all the family's belongings over a period of days. *Everything. Even the kitchen sink, and he tried to take the doors off the hinges!* I could not believe what I was hearing. Mama said that neighbors saw him taking things every day but did not do or say anything to stop him. He was discovered by Papa's brother but by then everything was taken.

They had no choice but to move in with Yeymi's grandmother, which is where they are now. So this precious family of six owns nothing in the world but a box of clothes and if the grandmother dies they will be forced to rely on the mercy of extended family members to stay in the house. Otherwise....

It's fair to say I was shell-shocked. I'd only ever heard of situations like this in the Compassion magazine or some distant documentary, but this was happening to my flesh and blood. We have been connected for two years through sponsorship–love, encouragement, letters and money and now God had brought us together to meet in person. Mayra, who works for Compassion, was almost in tears as she translated the sorry tale. Fortunately, Visit Hosts write a report of each visit and note any areas of concern, so she has the authority to intercede in this situation.

I am writing this only a matter of hours after experiencing it and I'm wrecked in heart, mind and spirit, but God has given me clarity to be able to communicate it.

I want to challenge you, particularly if you are a sponsor at the *'face-on-the-fridge-and-monthly-bill'* stage. It takes courage to move beyond this. But if you do, you will more clearly see the heart of God for His prized creation–people! It is a relationship, a two-way thing. Children want their parents and sponsors to be involved in their lives. A good start is writing regular letters. Your children *need* to hear from you, even the smallest thing. In many cases you are like a parent to them and are the only positive person in their life.

The danger of deliberately staying ignorant and disconnected from your sponsored child's reality is that you can become comfortable that you are doing a good thing and leave it at that. It can become about you. The one thing I can tell you after visiting so many of my kids is that in my own strength I alone am completely inadequate for the job of *releasing children from poverty in Jesus' name*. It is God alone who can release them and give them joy, hope, freedom and an opportunity to dream, despite their circumstances. I am merely an instrument He is using to show these precious people His love for them. There is nothing I'd rather be doing.

Visiting Mayra in Guatemala–Lessons Learned, Attitudes Adjusted
Friday 18 January 2013

I had really hoped today would be an easy day. After all, I wouldn't be going to see Mayra's house or community, so she could just forget her troubles and we could enjoy ourselves and have a great day. No deal. I was humbled and brought down today. Lessons were learned and attitudes were adjusted. After five child visits in which I was the 'main attraction,' where all the kids responded well to me and were animated and affectionate, today I took a back seat to the occasion.

10-year-old Mayra and her family of mum, dad and seven siblings live 300km to the north of Guatemala City and for some reason it takes nine hours by car. So it was decided that, rather than go all that way to visit her house and community, it would be better to bring her and her father to the City and we'd have a few hours at the zoo as a special treat.

When we met, I could tell Mayra was a troubled child and her life is hard. She was tired, cold, nervous, overwhelmed and scared. She had no eye contact, no smile, no response. Even though she knew I was her sponsor, all she saw was this strange white guy speaking a strange language, wearing a t-shirt and shorts in the cold weather, flashing around a big fat wallet and fancy phone (hey, I had to pay and take pics).

Spanish isn't the first language of Mayra's family. They are Mayan and they speak Q'eqchi, so that made my translator Big Mayra's job a fair bit harder. I could tell this day was not going to live up to 'my expectations' (like it's about me anyway?).

Neither Mayra nor her father had ever been to the zoo before. She wandered around and stared in awed silence as she saw every imaginable animal up close for the first time. I kept my distance during this time. Whereas the other kids would reach for my hand or put their arm around me, there were no such movements from Mayra.

Big Mayra did a great job of moving things along so we made the most of every minute. We saw lions, tigers, bears, elephants, giraffes, meerkats, monkeys, giant beavers, many kinds of birds, even an Australian section with kangaroos, wallabies and emus.

There was also a section of the park with rides, including a couple of rollercoasters, giant slide, trampolines and kiddie rides. I took her on the mini-rollercoaster and the giant slide, doing my best to coax or cajole some visible reaction of enthusiasm and joy out of her. While I'm sure she enjoyed herself, not once during the day did she show it on the outside.

At this point the attitude insidiously crept in—the disgusting, self-righteous attitude that silently demands groveling displays of thankfulness and gratitude for a good deed done, and judges and points fingers when none is forthcoming *"I'm doing all this for them, but...."* I felt sick and quickly moved on from those thoughts.

After the incredible rollercoaster that was the first five child visits, I thought maybe being away from Mayra's home and community may mean I wouldn't have to confront the harshness of her life and reality. I was wrong. The zoo and the city are obviously so far removed from their reality and both Mayra and her father were clearly in culture shock. During the day details of their lives came out in brief little tidbits and the more I heard, the more relieved I was that I didn't drive nine hours to see it. Just being brutally honest there.

Mayra's father told me his wife would have liked to come but someone had to be at home, otherwise their house would be broken into and people would take their stuff. *They can't even leave their house vacant without fear of being robbed!* Many houses in their community don't have proper floors, walls or beds. Mayra's father shared he has trouble affording to send her to school.

I was told in many Mayan communities women are still devalued and considered inferior, which would explain Mayra's demeanor—only speaking when spoken to and even then in one or two words, always looking to the ground. I only saw one or two smiles the whole day and even then it seemed like a real effort for her, like it wasn't a practised skill. In all honesty, from the little bit I heard of what her life is like, I don't think she has many reasons to smile.

There was a Pollo Campero at the Park (three times in three days!) so we shared lunch and then I gave Mayra some gifts for her and her family. The necklace with the 'Jesus' fish was quite fitting, because from what I learned of the family's situation He is the only hope they have.

There were a lot of unknowns and unanswered questions from our day together. We didn't really connect or engage. Was it a worthwhile exercise? So they've had a day at a zoo, now they go back to their same struggles and harsh reality, of which I still know very little, mainly because I was trying hard to not have to find out after yesterday. So that's my loss, I guess.

Mayra's father and Project director were both very thankful and expressed their gratitude several times. When we prayed, I left Mayra with 'The Blessing' from the book of Numbers chapter 6: *"May the Lord bless you and protect you. May the Lord smile on you and be gracious to you. May the Lord show you his favour and give you his peace."*

I learned from Big Mayra after we had left the park that Mayra's father had asked her to ask me for money to help his family. She wisely chose not to raise that issue with me in front of them. This 'direct canvassing' is strictly against Compassion's policies and for good reason. I felt quite awkward when I realized he had asked this and then watched me shell out the cash for their transport and accommodation.

How do I tie this up? I guess the reality check for me from today is that just because you invest in people, care for them and show them extravagant love doesn't mean they will always react the way you want or expect. That's part of being human and part of being in relationship with others. Grace, mercy and patience are needed.

This reminds me of God's love for us. Imagine if He got grumpy with us every time we didn't respond to His limitless acts of love for us. There would be no-one left! We, then, need to treat others the same.

Visiting Rosa and Katherine in El Salvador

Re-visiting Rosa in El Salvador–A Family Reunion
Monday 21 January 2013
Excuse the hyperbole, but today was sent to me straight from heaven! In contrast to some of my other stories it's vast-majority 'sweetness and light' today, folks.

In 2007 I started sponsoring 7-year-old Rosa and in 2009 I ventured over to Chinameca, El Salvador to visit her and her family when she was a shy 9-year-old. This visit was actually the motivation I needed to start writing regular letters, because that's what the kids really need and want. I could see how disappointed she was that I had only written a few letters, so I resolved to change and started writing monthly to my many Compassion kids.

Rosa has a Mama, Papa, older stepsister Vanesa (18), twin sister Ester and younger brother Josue (10). Unfortunately Vanesa couldn't be with us. Papa told us she had really been looking forward to seeing me again but she had received the call at 9.00pm the previous night to go and work at the little shop which is her place of employment. Vanesa was never sponsored but she still has ambitions to have a career and she is using this job to try and pay her way through University.

Normally on a sponsor visit the Project is the first stop, but since today was the first day of school for the year and there was no Project action in the morning, we went to the family's house first. It was interesting going back a second time. A lot of the conversation revolved around what had happened in the last three years for both of us and what had changed. We reminisced over what we remembered about the last visit. The family knew a lot about me and take great interest in my letters.

I still learned some new things about the family today. I learned the kids have to get up really early to get to school, which starts at 7.30am, because there's 49 kids in Rosa's class and if they get there late they get a seat up the back and can't hear very well. The kids all have dreams related to the medical profession (doctor, nurse, clinical lab technician) and are currently achieving good grades. Rosa and Ester have only just started 7th grade but the family is already talking LDP (*Leadership Development Program, in which a select group of Compassion-sponsored kids are then sponsored through College and raised up to become Christian leaders of their communities and countries*).

Rosa's parents make money by making and selling a traditional drink called Horchata. The recipe has been passed down through the family and it is indeed a 'family business.' When the kids aren't at school or the Compassion Project they help their parents sell it. They spend all morning preparing it, go out on the streets with a couple of buckets full and sell it in plastic bags. On a good day in the warm weather they make $20. In the cooler weather, they don't make much. Mama has a couple of other job options for lean times, such as cleaning houses or helping make and sell a traditional El Salvador food called pupusas. I had three today, and they were delicious. The family's house is adequate and belonged to their parents, so they are blessed to not have to pay any rent.

The ambition, optimism and dreams of this family is mind-blowing and breathtaking considering their circumstances, but it comes purely and simply from their unshakeable contentment, joy, faith and trust in Jesus. I felt so blessed to be connected to this family. Papa took us out the back and showed us the process for making horchata. The family's menagerie of animals was still there from last time: a cat, a couple of dogs, some chickens, and a green Australian parakeet.

After a wonderful conversation, gift giving and recreating the family photo out the front of the house, we headed out to San Miguel for some lunch. I received some 'respite' from Pollo Campero (not that I needed it) because Rosa likes pizza, so just like the first visit back in 2009 we went to Pizza Hut. After lunch it was time to return to Project ES718.

Project visits are always a joy and this was no exception. Last time I was here it was El Salvador Children's Day, so things were quite chaotic, with piñatas and candy flying everywhere. Today was a lot more relaxed. We were greeted by the children in a guard of honor, some holding red, blue and white streamers. We went upstairs to a big room where they welcomed me. I introduced myself and showed them the Australian football, they sang a couple of songs to me and I played 'Blessed Be Your Name' and 'Open the Eyes of My Heart' on an unfortunately out-of-tune guitar. The kids then went off to their classes.

Rosa and Ester are nearly 13 and enjoy the same things as most girls their age. The Project offers a Cosmetology workshop (hair, nails, manicures, pedicures etc.) for the girls, and I understand some of the girls who have done it in the past have successfully earned an income out of it. So an important part of what Compassion does is offer the kids, and often the parents, income-generating skills to help lift themselves out of poverty.

In a very special time I was able to meet and talk to the group of girls, aged 13-15, who were doing the cosmetology workshop. We traded questions and answers, and of course the question came up about whether I was married or had a girlfriend. Answer: No. Moving on thanks... I was privileged to be able to lift up this group of girls to God and pray for them on behalf of their sponsors. We went around the circle and they shared prayer requests. Most of them kept it fairly basic, but I was honored that they'd only just met me and were willing to share things that were happening in their lives. I prayed about their families, friends, studies, sponsors, and that they would make wise decisions about their lives as they got older.

After this it was play time. We went out on the street, kicked the footy and the soccer ball, jumped a skipping rope and had races. I did much more than my knees were happy with. We finished with a special time of eating pupusas and drinking way too much orange drink with just Rosa's family and a couple of the Project staff. The Project staff shared about the massive impact the sponsors have on their children, particularly through the letters and visits. I'm continually amazed at the reaction I get from kids who don't even know me, who speak a different language and who I would have thought may be a little bit scared of this bald, bearded guy. They just love having a sponsor there and it doesn't matter if it's their sponsor or not. That's how much it means to them.

I was also honored to be able to pray for and encourage each family member and the Project workers who were there. I will never cease to be amazed and inspired by Compassion Project workers. Every person who works for Compassion is an incredible servant of God and their stories need to be told. They give their lives for the kids and their families in the name of bringing them the love of Jesus.

Because the driver, Jorge my translator and I were staying in San Miguel, I was able to spend more time with the family and didn't have to rush off. We ended up leaving at 5.00pm, which made for a tiring but rewarding and positive day.

Visiting Katherine in El Salvador
Poverty of Family and Hope for the Future
Tuesday 22 January 2013
I saw true courage today. The courage of a Mama trying to hold her marriage together for the sake of her children and future generations. The courage of a couple sharing their struggles so personally with someone they just met. I also displayed courage today. The courage to ask hard questions of a woman I'd just met, not knowing how or if she'd respond. The result of this courage was that I now know this family on a whole new level and I'm starting to get a true picture of just how significant a sponsor is, not just to the child but to the whole family.

At breakfast, my Compassion host and translator Jorge shared with me some interesting things about poverty in El Salvador. While the physical poverty is evident everywhere, the deeper issue is 'poverty of family.' A significant percentage of marriages are disintegrating and as a result the children do not feel secure, safe or loved. This goes on for generations. I took it on board and stored it in the memory bank.

Little did I know I would soon be face-to-face with this poverty of family in an incredibly personal way. I have been sponsoring 6-year-old Katherine for a year. She's one of the newer additions to my Compassion family. Katherine lives with Mama, Papa and her older brother Tony (11) in the east of El Salvador.

Today's visit was going to be short, due to having to drive three-and-a-half hours back to San Salvador to catch a plane. Therefore I wanted to make every minute count. I had to quickly catch and destroy my local 'Negative Attitude Monster' when we didn't get to the Project until 9.30am.

Katherine's Project has been operating for five years. They started with 150 kids and now have 266, aged 3-14. The Project Director is a friendly young guy who loves what he does and clearly has the respect of the children and families.

I was welcomed by a relatively small contingent of children in the church, since it was a school day. This didn't matter one bit, as I still felt very loved and accepted. There were red, white and blue streamers and balloons around the place (seems to be a common theme) and "*Very Welcome Mr. David Chalmers*" was projected onto a wall.

I met Katherine and she presented me with a foam square painted like the Australian flag with outlines of her hands on the back. Some children recited Bible memory verses then I introduced myself, taught them to say "*G'day Australia!*" as well as jump like a kangaroo and sleep like a koala. They invited me to get on the drums (to which I never say no) so I had a quick bash while they clapped along. A little guy who would have been about 10 also got on the drums and did a very good job.

We then went on a quick tour of the Project and met kids and staff. There was a lot of construction and extension work going on, which indicates growth. The staff told me about the programs run by this particular Project. I've found it interesting how each Project has a different focus in terms of the activities, skills or workshops offered. This Project has three main workshops aimed at giving kids income-generating skills for the future: bakery, computer class and 'electricity' was how the third one was translated to me. I can only assume it's to do with basic engineering or fixing things.

The next stop was Katherine's home. I was pleased to hear that the neighborhood is considered very safe and they have no real problems with gangs. In the house they have a front living area with a large hammock stretched across it. There is one bedroom and the 'kitchen' is outside, on what we might call the back veranda or patio. Except it's definitely not a patio. The roof is made from iron sheets, held down with rocks and whatever other heavy objects they can find. The backyard is a courtyard filled with crud and shared with three or four other houses. There are two 'toilets' to share. These are basically hollowed-out concrete blocks which are raised up in order to be able to sit on them. I don't recall seeing a door in front of either toilet. They have running water but it's incredibly unreliable. When we visited, they hadn't had water for *two days*! When I heard that I thanked God that both kids in the family are registered and sponsored through Compassion.

Papa was not there when I visited. He earns a three-figure monthly wage working as a cleaner/security guy at the local school, where Katherine is about to start First Grade. There's a bit of symmetry there, since I was also about to start teaching First Grade. I understand Mama does not contribute financially to the family at the moment but she told me she sometimes makes and sells tortillas.

For lunch, Katherine chose Pollo Campestre, which is the El Salvador version of Pollo Campero (from Guatemala, but also in El Salvador). Every three months the Project takes the kids there for birthday celebrations. On the way there we did something that wasn't in the schedule but turned out to be incredibly significant. We stopped at the school to meet and talk to Papa. We met outside the front gate which he initially left open. In no time, half a dozen faces had appeared and he motioned for them to get back inside. Apparently some of the students like to try and escape so, seeing the open gate, thought they'd seize their opportunity. Papa is in his mid-30s and seems like a nice guy, though I can imagine him being quite intimidating if you got on the wrong side of him.

We talked about his job and then asked for prayer requests for the family. The reply came "*Please pray for my family. My wife and I sometimes fight.*" I was taken aback, but appreciated his honesty and made sure I told him this. Later, as we were sitting in the children's area of Pollo Campestre, I wondered how I was going to follow this up with Mama, or even if I should.

Lunch was okay, though not as good as Pollo Campero. We traded questions and the conversation flowed. Mama was beautiful and engaging. I asked Tony some questions and found out that he is in 6th Grade, he wants to be a professional football player and his favorite player is Lionel Messi (not a bad choice). He has sponsors from the US who he hears from regularly.

I gave out gifts to the family and I'm pretty sure the other patrons of the children's area of Pollo Campestre were wondering what was going on at our table, and where they could get a necklace, teddy bear, Australian flag and snow globe, among other things.

Mama started talking about her relationship with her husband. They got together 13 years ago when she was at school. She was selling bread at the same time, to raise enough money to keep going to school. She said she always knew, when school finished, "*The bread was waiting.*" Papa laid eyes on her and it was 'love at first sight.' Ah yes, that old chestnut. He did not attend the school but would go in just to see her. They are together all these years later, but one gets the sense all is not well.

Finally, when the two kids were off playing, those remaining at the table were Mama and three males. Me, Jorge (host) and the Project Director. I decided to ask the question.

"Your husband said that you and he fight a bit. Can I ask what you fight about?"

"*He's seeing another woman.*"

Silence. Me: "But he's married to you?"

"*Yes.*"

Me: Baffled silence. Then: "I'm just trying to understand how that works." This was 'poverty of family' come alive right before my eyes.

Questions go round in the head. Scenarios, solutions. The reality that she couldn't really leave him at this point even if she wanted to (not that that would be the best solution), because he's the one financially contributing to the family and selling tortillas is not going to provide for two children.

I look at Mama. She is strong, patient and understanding. I would also add brave and courageous for sharing it with us. Three males, two of whom she's only just met.

It's a testimony to the trust she has in the Project Director, who has built a relationship with the family over the five years they've been involved with the Compassion Project.

It's also a testimony to the trust she has in me, her daughter's sponsor, who speaks words of love and encouragement into her life and loves them enough to travel halfway round the world to see them and *be with* them.

"*I am fighting for my marriage for the sake of my children; setting an example for them.*" I learned that Mama's parents were in the same situation. This 'poverty of family' is a generational thing in El Salvador but Mama is determined it will stop here.

With God's help and Compassion's support, it can. But there is one more step they need to take. Tony listed his favorite Project activity as 'learning about God.' Katherine, being a life-loving, enthusiastic six-year-old, loves everything about the Project, especially the God-stuff – singing songs and learning the Bible. However, to my knowledge neither Mama nor Papa have fully committed themselves to the church or to Jesus. Yet. That is the Great Unknown. Or, depending on how you look at it, with their two kids being cared for like they are with Compassion, the Great Inevitable.

I'm not suggesting that by becoming Christians all their marriage problems will instantly disappear. Being 'perpetually single' I'm no expert on marriage, but I'm pretty safe in saying that marriage requires hard work on both sides. Papa has a decision to make in regards to committing completely to his wife.

However, the first thing I thought of when I got in the car after saying goodbye was the incredible contrast between the two families I visited in the last two days. Both families live in El Salvador. Both families have children sponsored and supported through Compassion. Both families are in economical and living situations which are 'not real flash.'

Here's the difference: In Rosa's home, which was one of the rare visits where I went away with my heart completely full and joyous, I felt love, joy, peace, dreams, positive ambitions and contentment. This is due to one simple fact. They are a committed Christian family with an incredible faith and trust in God to provide for them and are part of a church community. That's where their Hope lies.

And that's what I believe is missing from Katherine's family. Mama and Papa both love their kids but when the marriage is not strong, the family disintegrates. And trying to fix broken relationships is the sort of problem that if you try in your own strength you will fail. If they really want to solve their conflicts in a way that won't lead to a continuation of the 'poverty of family' they need to commit their lives, marriage and family to Jesus.

If I had not come to visit, I would not have known any of this. In a short time we went deep. I had the courage to ask hard questions and Mama had the courage to answer them. I am now better equipped to pray, and trust that God will work in the lives of the family. The final decision lies with them.

Visiting Jacqueline In Ecuador—A Day of Pure Joy and Learning About Trust
Saturday 26 January 2013

'Trust in the Lord with all your heart; do not depend on your own understanding. Seek His will in all you do, and He will direct your paths.' (Proverbs 3:5-6)

For Christians, these words are very well known and we do our best to live by them. But how often do we really trust God *with all our heart* or acknowledge Him *in all our ways*? I sure don't as much as I would like. When I was in Ecuador in late January visiting my Compassion sponsored child Jacqueline, I caught a glimpse of what it really means to trust fully and completely and I want to share it with you.

I'm so glad I went to Ecuador. When I planned my trip to Central America in January, I wasn't originally going to include Ecuador because it was a little bit 'out of the way' compared to the other countries I planned to visit. I have been sponsoring 6-year-old Jacqueline for two-and-a half years and it was her letters that got me. Here is a sample:

– *I would like to meet you because I would like to know you and your toys*

– *Jacqueline loves you, and for her, the wish to know you is the most beautiful in her life*

– *She also wonders if you will be able to meet face to face someday*

– *She wants you to know that she would like to know you in some moment to share with you nice moments*

– *Do you know something incredible? You are a hero for Jacque, she would like to be like you when she grows up – a great professional. She wants to work with children, and the same as you, to be mature spiritually in faith. Jacque wants that you never get apart from Jesus. Jacque would like to be like you because you follow Jesus Christ's footprints. Jacque asks God that you come to Ecuador. She wants to see your eyes and tell you she loves you*

Alright, alright, I get the hint! So Ecuador was included in the itinerary. I say it again, I'm so glad I went to Ecuador. It was one of the few days on the trip that I didn't leave with some sort of heartbreak or negative feeling. And that's not because her family's life isn't hard. They're a family of seven at risk of being turfed out of their house, and the jobs of her parents are anything but secure or lucrative.

However what I found was, because of some of the situations I experienced that wrecked me, God multiplied the impact of the joyous moments. And this day was *joyous*. I reveled in Jacqueline's pure innocence, joy and excitement.

We met in the foyer of my hotel–Jacqueline, her mum, her Project Director and my translator. I wasn't sure what sort of reaction I'd get from Jacqueline but she turned out to be one of the more affectionate and open of my children right from the start. On another trip I visited an 18-year-old who didn't say "boo" and now I had this six-year-old who chatted away.

She was tiny like a doll, and she squeezed her way into my heart right away. The visit took place on a Saturday and our first stop was an amusement park in the city of Quito. We loaded up a prepaid card with $40 and off we went. Jacqueline was, to paraphrase my friend Homer Simpson, *"like a kid in some kind of a store."* For whatever reason, she particularly liked the rides that did nothing but go round and round. We had a jolly old time on merry-go-rounds, giant slides, trampolines, mini-pirate ship and even the waste-of-money sideshow games (though on this day not one cent was wasted).

I was able to go on some rides with her. To share this time with a precious little girl who was enjoying what many people consider to be standard childhood experiences for the first time was an amazing privilege, and more than once I got lost in the moment.

During our morning together, Jacqueline was running purely on adrenalin and excitement. Her Mama shared with me that she hadn't slept very well the previous night since she was so excited, and I could see her getting gradually more tired. She made it through lunch, then we travelled an hour to her home. During this time, Jacqueline finally succumbed and fell asleep. *In my arms.*

I cannot describe the significance of that moment. God was showing me His love for Jacqueline and His love for me. This was Proverbs 3:5-6 come to life. To me, falling asleep in someone's arms is the greatest example of trust we can demonstrate as humans. We make ourselves totally vulnerable and our lives are completely in the other person's hands. Jacqueline was showing me that she trusted me with all her heart and God was whispering to me *"This is how I want My people to trust Me."* Lesson learned.

Trust is something that takes a long time to earn but only a moment to lose. Every day I am thankful for the little people God has entrusted to me to educate, encourage and love over the last few years-students, nieces, nephews, Compassion kids and kids who have been abandoned and orphaned. It is equally a privilege and a responsibility that I don't take lightly.

Visiting Antonio in Nicaragua-The Turning Point
Friday 25 January 2013

During my January trip I visited 3 kids in Nicaragua and it was difficult. It was stinking hot, the driver got lost on all three days and my translator was frustrating, in that I sometimes had to prompt her to actually translate for me.

The part that stood out to me was my visit to Antonio. This 8-year-old kid was full of life. Chatty, talkative, animated. We hung out at the church for a while, drank coke and played with my Australian football.

In contrast I noticed his mother, who looked so young and was nursing a brand new baby, didn't say a word. Even in our conversations she almost had to be prompted. I sensed much sadness and loneliness in her life.

I took Antonio, his cousin and a few other relatives out to a chicken restaurant for lunch and they continued to talk, and talk, and sing, and talk. We had a ball. Then it was time to visit the family home.

Antonio's home visit was probably the hardest I had done to that point. It was *The Turning Point*, as I have entitled this story. The house was nothing more than a brick box. Dirt floor, holes in the roof. One bedroom. No privacy or dignity for this woman with an 8-year-old and a new baby.

We sat around and chatted for a while. The conversation was driven by the Project workers since I was lost for words, taking in everything around me, and I still sensed Mama's sadness and shyness. We got Antonio talking, I showed him some pictures and gave him some gifts. When I do a home visit I can normally ask to take photos of the house, and can manage an *"Oh, this is lovely!"* even when I'm churning inside and thinking *"How do they live like this, day after day?"* Today I just couldn't do it. It just didn't feel right.

I learned that Mama was 23, so she was just 15 when she had Antonio. Antonio's father left just after he was born and she now had a husband who was as young, if not younger, than she was. He scratches an income selling newspapers at the local market.

The Turning Point came when we ventured out into the backyard, and I use that term loosely. It was a dump, with a cinder block out in the open for a toilet. At this point everything that had been building up inside me as I learned about their reality came crashing down. I felt the full force of their despair and hopelessness. I could not move. I had no words.

After a couple of minutes I managed to speak: "*Jesus. Jesus.*" Over and over again, that was all I could say.

The next few minutes were holy, sacred and powerful. I did the only thing I could think of. I held this beautiful young woman and I prayed for her. I lifted her up to God. God gave me the words and He gave me the strength to say them. Mama was overcome. Her brokenness was evident, but as I prayed I could feel her responding and crying out to God in her spirit.

The Bible says God's strength and power is made perfect in our weakness (2 Cor. 12:9), and it was certainly true on this day. This was 'The Turning Point' because God helped me to truly realize that without Him we have nothing. I guess I knew this in theory but my wealth, prosperity, abundance, self-reliance and self-sufficiency prevented me from knowing it fully.

People who are materially poor know what it is to depend on God and trust Him completely. They have to. This is a great example to me and I know God wanted me to see all these things for this exact reason.

I want to live a life that demonstrates complete trust, dependence and reliance on God. I don't want material possessions or a life of comfort and ease to stand in the way of my relationship with God.

As heartbreaking as this day with Antonio and his family was, God has put two sparkles of blessing in their lives: Compassion and Antonio's grandmother. Without Compassion, Antonio wouldn't have regular food, clean water, education or medical care. Even though Antonio's father left, his grandmother stayed. I was inspired by the love and care Antonio's grandmother has for him, despite technically having no obligation to. This is the Love of God in action.

Journey #4–Philippines, April 2013

Around the same time as I was organizing my Central America 'mega-tour' in November 2012, I received an email about a Compassion Insight trip to the Philippines in April 2013, which just happened to fall in the school holidays. It also just so happened that I sponsored three kids in the Philippines, so I thought "*Why not?*" God had provided me with both health and finances. This trip was a group tour visiting several Compassion Projects, churches and homes to get a 'behind-the-scenes' look at what Compassion does and the impact that it has. We would also get to meet our sponsored kids. I had never done a group tour before and I knew it would be very different to what I had experienced previously. I was right.

To be devastatingly honest, I didn't think a whole lot about the Philippines trip until two days before I was due to get on the plane. I read what I needed to read and I paid what I needed to pay, but there were other things going on. What I saw and experienced during the 3-week Central/South America trip in January really messed me up and consumed me for months afterward. I also started a job at a new school two days after I returned and moved house four days before the trip. We had parent-teacher interviews in the previous two weeks and I had lost my voice and wasn't feeling that crash-hot.

So it was with a suitably reserved and subdued sense of anticipation that I boarded a plane at 1am on a Saturday morning, and headed off to meet my teammates. Our team consisted of 12 people and two leaders from five different states of Australia, very few of whom had actually met face-to-face before. We had three online teleconferences before we left and I was only able to get on one of them, because I was either in the Dominican Republic or in Parent-Teacher interviews. Surely it would take a miracle for this thing to work?

My original plan was to visit my three sponsored kids Cashofia (7), John Dave (8) and Princess Joy (12), who live on three different islands, at their homes and Projects in the first week of the holidays, then join the rest of the team in Manila for the group tour in the second week. However, as the Central America trip progressed, with the amount of money I was spending and the fact I was officially unemployed during this time, it was apparent that this would not work. So I figured it would be better instead to fly them up to Manila for the child-sponsor visit day. Princess Joy, in particular, often referred in her letters to the fact they were very poor and couldn't afford or do basic things, so I figured this would be a life-changing experience for her.

Because I was the only team member from Victoria I flew to Singapore separately to the others, which gave me a nice little 11-hour stopover at Changi airport. A bit annoying, you might think, but with the gift of perspective I tell you the truth, there are many worse places you could be stuck in transit than Changi Airport. I finally met up with the team and we made our way to Manila.

We were a motley crew and at first glance it was a combination unlikely to jell. Strangers, really. Fourteen people from five states of Australia. A 60-40 advantage to those aged over 50. Nine women, five men. Two couples, one mother-son combo, one pregnant woman and the rest of us had come alone, whether single or married. What we had in common: we sponsored kids in the Philippines, we love Compassion and wanted to see God do something amazing. What united us proved to be bigger than our differences.

This trip presented a number of challenges for me. I'll come right out and say it: I am essentially not a people-person. I am not really social and I am more task-oriented. I relate to people better when we're doing stuff together instead of sitting together at a café and just chatting. I'm the sort of person at an eat-and-chat gathering who ends up playing with the kids rather than engaging with adults. Conversation is not one of my favorite things.

I guess I could also be considered a 'seasoned traveler.' An early source of frustration for me was in the fact that a fair number of this team were first-time international travelers. When you're in a group of 14 it is impossible to stay out of the way of others, but it is exacerbated when people are just standing there, looking around and unaware of their surroundings. God gave me grace and patience, and I bit my tongue and resisted saying potentially harmful things to team members several times.

I have to say that on this occasion I enjoyed being a 'sheep.' Having someone else in charge of the itinerary telling me where I needed to be and what I needed to do. Someone else having the responsibility of guiding and leading. Karl and Lil did this very well, I might add, and I couldn't do their job for quids.

Overall I concluded that, when travelling, I still like to be in control. In sync with my 'lone ranger' personality I like to know where I'm going and when I'm going to get there, which I can do much better on an individual trip rather than travelling in a group.

It was also very different for me visiting Compassion Projects and homes with which I had no personal connection. In which I wasn't the 'center of attention.' While that may sound egotistical, it's not meant to. On each of my previous trips, because it was an individual visit, my presence was the main focus. I enjoyed this and basically had the floor. I have either sung, played guitar, drums or piano at every Project I have been to, whereas on these trips I took on more of a background role as part of a team. I still had an amazing time and I was still able to engage with many people during the Project visits on this trip. I'm not saying they were better or worse experiences, just different than what I was used to.

During the trip, the team was also privileged to visit the homes of Compassion-supported families. All my previous visits were to the homes of my Compassion-sponsored kids, so there was that extra level of significance and personal connection. Having said that, I know that the rest of the team and I were always incredibly impacted by these home visits. Despite the circumstances many of them lived in, they always displayed such joy, contentment, gratitude, generosity and hospitality that came from their faith in God and the assistance that Compassion was giving their family.

With all the travel I have done with Compassion and the experiences and knowledge I have gained, it would have been very easy for me to go into this trip with an attitude of superiority and 'know-it-all-ism.' I know it was there at the start, at least internally. Whether it seeped out, you would have to ask the other team members.

I have to say that I was so inspired and encouraged by my fellow team members, however inexperienced they may have been compared to me in terms of Compassion trips or experiences. One couple had been sponsoring a girl for 12 years since she was very young and got to meet the now-18-year-old on this trip. They had recently sold a property and planned to use the freed-up money to sponsor more kids and go on more trips. Now that they had seen first-hand what an impact we can have as sponsors, and Compassion has, they are so well-equipped to inspire and encourage others to make a difference.

Another couple's young adult son severely injured his ankle and had to have surgery in the week before the trip. They had arranged to meet their sponsored girl in the week before the tour but this had thrown their plans into disarray. Fortunately for all the team, God made a way and they were able to do the visit and then come on the tour, which was a blessing for all of us.

There was also a young 20-year-old guy who came with his mum and stepped massively out of his comfort zone to experience a different world, engaged with people he might not usually associate with and impressed everyone with his gift of photography.

I love being with people who are as passionate about Compassion as I am and this was the main reason I wanted to go on the trip. There were so many inspiring and encouraging moments and we all concluded that only God could bring together 14 strangers from different parts of the country and create such a cohesive group. The experiences we shared were God-sent and will always connect us.

One thing was clear, and was confirmed by our trip leader Lil. Every person on this team loved and effectively engaged with every person we met. We showed them the love of God, if only for a painfully short time. With my experience of what I call the 'little pockets of heaven' a.k.a Compassion Projects, I personally can't imagine going to one and not engaging, but according to Lil she's led groups where the members have initially stood back and struggled to get involved. No such problems on this trip. In many cases we were also the first group or the first people to visit the Project, which was quite significant and a privilege.

Two guys I have to mention are Ian and Cromwell. Ian is the Tour and Visit Specialist for Compassion Philippines. He basically organizes every detail of the group tours. He was with us the whole time and went out of his way to accommodate us and make sure we had everything we need. In his 'spare time' he was also organizing a trip that was to happen the next week. Ian was an amazing blessing from God and we were all thankful to have him.

Cromwell has been working for Compassion Philippines for 25 years and loves his job. He is the Partnership Facilitator (PF) for the region that we were visiting, which included the island of Bohol. The PF is in charge of coordinating a number of Projects and visiting them, making sure everything is running as it should. Cromwell travelled with us for most of the trip and was an absolute delight. His insight into the area and the way Compassion works was invaluable and at each Project you could tell the respect he commanded, as well as his heart for the children and staff. He and I connected and enjoyed a couple of late night walks in the stifling heat to local coffee establishments.

Philippines Day 1–PH954 (Child Survival Program)
Sunday 7 April 2013
Our first day was hectic and non-stop from start to finish. Looking back, if this had been my first overseas adventure I don't know how I would have coped, so I salute my travelling companions for making it through. Having spent the night in Manila, we began the day with another flight to an island 800km south east, called Bohol, where we would spend the next four days.

Bohol was a massive contrast to the hustle and bustle of Manila. There was less traffic and less crime, which made two big ticks in my book. Once we got off the plane, we headed straight for a Compassion Project. This is the name given to the place where sponsored children (and often parents) meet to receive food, education, medical care, love, encouragement and, most importantly, the opportunity for a relationship with Jesus. Each Project has a unique identification code based on its location and when it is registered.

During our trip we were privileged to visit four Compassion Projects, in a combination of urban and rural areas. We also visited the homes of four families connected with the Projects, toured the Compassion Office in Manila and met with six LDP (Leadership Development Program) students and hear their stories.

The procedure for when we arrived at each place was pretty much standard.
- We arrived to a sea of beautiful, happy faces.
- Handshakes, hugs and high-fives followed, as we made our way into the church.
- There were a couple of testimonies from a parent and a child.
- The Project director and Pastor spoke.
- There were some songs and performances from the kids and/or parents.
- We finished with a performance from our group, which was led by me.

I made it clear from the start that I was happy to take a leading role in this area, having spent years as a music teacher. Also, a summer at Camp Tecumseh in Indiana in 2004 had given me an impressive repertoire of fun kid's songs, some of which transcended language barriers. We had our first practise on the bus ten minutes before arriving at the Project. Fortunately, this group was quite willing to abandon their inhibitions and make it fun for kids and adults alike. We performed 'My God is So Big' but the centerpiece and our unofficial theme song was an action song called 'Baking a Cake' which I have now taught to children in 13 countries.

The Project we visited on this day was called PH954, and we were here to observe the Child Survival Program (CSP) in action. At this Project a group of mothers performed a dance to the song 'One Way, Jesus.' The toddler son of one of the mums came up on stage, trying to get her attention. He then brought a plastic chair on stage and somehow got it stuck around his neck. He was taken care of by one of the Project workers while the mum continued the dance, so keen was she to preserve her dignity and not disrupt the performance. Thankfully there was a happy ending and the little guy was okay.

After the official proceedings were over it was now time to mingle. The team was divided into three groups to enable us to interact with the mothers of the CSP and their babies. We witnessed them doing a cooking class as well as making bags from cereal boxes, which they are able to sell to earn some money for themselves to provide for their family. Normally they use a sewing machine to put the bags together but the machine was broken, so they were sewing by hand.

I'll be honest and say that this session was way out of my comfort zone and I took a long time to engage. I'm a single guy and although I have nieces and nephews, engaging with women and very little kids of a different language and culture just seemed beyond my capabilities. I just didn't feel like I could go up and start a conversation with them. Fortunately the women of our group did a fantastic job of engaging and connecting with the mums and babies. I was in awe.

Eventually I got over myself and sat down next to a mum making a recycled-cereal-box-bag. I started a conversation with her and her shy friend and it turned out I had chosen the cheekiest delight of a woman to engage with. Of course we ended up playing a guessing game about my age and then I faced the inevitable questions as to why I wasn't married. I have become used to this by now, but my singleness at age 31 was greeted with particular surprise in the Philippines more than any other country I have visited.

After this it was time for a home visit and we were once again divided into three groups. My group visited the home of the father who had shared his testimony at the church. I continue to shake my head at the courage of this man. The family, whose oldest son is sponsored, live in an elevated bamboo hut. I was invited inside the house but I didn't stay in for long. The floor was also made of bamboo and in my running shoes I felt like I would fall through the floor. I know Filipinos are generally smaller but I can't imagine the logistics of six people living in that house. This family was so friendly, gracious at our presence and so thankful for the difference God was using Compassion to make in their lives.

My group also visited another family who lived two doors away. The very young mum-of-four is part of the CSP. What struck me was her joy. They don't have running water or walls on their house, but our hosts were cheerful and friendly, and our conversation was punctuated by giggles and cackles of laughter. This is purely the result of the hope that the help of Compassion gives.

That night we were able to attend the evening service of the church connected with the Project we had visited that day. One thing that was hard for me to get used to was people just chatting away during the service and during the ceremony at the Project. We consider it a lack of respect but that's just the way they do things. The music was great, led by an all-female team of five and the instruments were all up the back, high on the balcony. I had never seen that before. The message was hard to sit through, with the speaker effortlessly switching between English and his local dialect.

After church we enjoyed a meal with some of the Compassion staff from PH954.

Philippines Day 2-PH961, Word of Hope Church, Bohol
Monday 8 April, 2013
After the awkwardness of Day 1, struggling to relate to and connect with mums and bubs, I was in my element today. We were visiting a Child Development Sponsorship Program (CDSP) which caters for school-aged kids. The Project we visited today, PH961, is relatively new. It started in 2006 and the oldest kids are around 12-13 years old. We learned that the area has a low crime rate and is not really affected by natural disasters.

We learned that the three people in charge of this church and Project have high influence in the community. One is a Dean of a local University and another is in local government. The kids at this Project were on vacation at this time but they put on a special day to accommodate our visit. We were told that we were the first group of sponsors to visit the Project. They also had 30 children recently registered, but not sponsored. We would get the opportunity to meet, play with and hopefully find these kids a sponsor.

We also learned that this Project has a special Australian connection. Last year PH961 was visited by an Australian sponsor and her friend, who was not a sponsor. The friend was so moved by what she experienced, when she got back to Australia she arranged a substantial four-figure monetary gift for the Project, which they used to build more classrooms.

Once again we were welcomed by a sea of smiling, friendly faces wearing yellow shirts. There was a song and a couple of testimonies. We performed our songs.

After this we split into three groups to tour the Project and see the classrooms. The kids were busy drawing and writing letters to their sponsors. I took the Australian football around and tried to engage the kids with my usual engagement tools: thumb wrestling, paper/scissors/rock, finger trick. Many of the kids were very shy because of the language barrier. The group I was with just before lunch were a bit more open, so I taught them a couple more songs.

Lunch was a fine spread; a feast of local seafood among other things. We were definitely left satisfied. After lunch the Project Director shared with us details of the way Compassion works and what's required of them. We saw financial records and children's files, which included health and medical records, school grades, details of letters and gifts received from sponsors. I switched off at this point because I'd seen it all before on my previous travels. I need no more convincing of Compassion's integrity.

After lunch we had free time with the kids. My Australian football (red and egg-shaped) was a huge success, particularly with the 3-5 year olds, whose throwing and catching skills astounded me. At one stage I had to share the footy between three groups—older boys who were competing for it, 3-5 year olds who simply wanted to throw and catch, and a bunch of girls off to the side. Other team members engaged the kids with things they brought such as bubbles, beach balls, parachutes and chalk.

Once again we ventured out on a home visit. We met a family with mum, dad and four kids. The sponsored child of the family was Jessa Mae, who is 12 or 13 and dreams of being a nurse. The parents are very proud of their kids and their medals of achievement are prominently displayed in the family home—a bamboo hut with separate rooms and an ordinary roof. The area is susceptible to flooding so they have a room built in that is slightly higher than the others. There have been occasions where they had to move all the family's possessions into this higher room. What I love is that the Compassion-assisted kids actually have dreams and realistically believe they can achieve them with God's help.

Philippines Day 3–5
PH959, Chocolate Hills, Compassion Office, Meet LDP Students
Tuesday, Wednesday and Thursday April 9-11

Tuesday was a very similar day. We visited a Project and witnessed so much joy, gratitude and generosity. We sang, played, engaged and loved. We met another batch of very young registered-but-unsponsored children. Who knows what they must have been thinking, confronted by these big white strangers bringing smiles, bubbles, balls, chalk and big colorful parachutes.

The footy was a big hit, once again with the little ones. One of my favorite moments involved a 4-year-old girl who wouldn't have anything to do with the bubbles that were being blown, but as soon as I put the football in her hands her eyes lit up like it was Christmas and she was at peace with the world. It was a good feeling having one of the mothers I had never met coming and asking me to be in a photo, rather than me having to cajole a smile out of these bewildered kids.

Our home visit today was special, profound and as an added bonus we got fed! The mama's rice cakes were delish (and washed down with Coke). I certainly wasn't going to refuse that hospitality. The house was very well put together, which we learned was the result of several family gifts from the young fella's very generous sponsor. We were so impressed with this kid. He was 'bright as a button' and dreams of being an engineer. You could taste the family's pride and expectation of a brighter future thanks to the help of Compassion.

The prayer time with the staff of this Project was very impacting and emotional for everyone involved. We felt a tangible sense of God's hand on the place and we were excited about what He would do with them in the future. We left confident in the knowledge that these kids and their families are being amazingly well looked after by the heroes that work for Compassion.

On the way back we stopped at a tourist attraction, a group of mountains called the Chocolate Hills. Apparently it's a 'must-see' in Bohol. So we saw the hills. On the bus afterward we learned about four of the myths or legends about how they came to be. Much to our amusement, two of the stories involved Giants pooping, and the resulting excrement turned out to be the Chocolate Hills. Lovely.

On Thursday we said goodbye to Bohol and flew back to Manila. Our first stop was the Compassion Office, where we were able to talk to staff, see the different departments and get a really good behind-the-scenes look at the 'engine room' where the action happens. What I loved was the number of Compassion staff who used to be sponsored kids. The more stories I hear like that, the more I am affirmed and encouraged that this thing *works*! One guy in particular went from sponsored child, to LDP graduate, to Pastor, to Project Director, to working in the Compassion Office. The lady who registered him all those years ago also works in the Office. You can't make this stuff up!

In the evening we had dinner with six students of the Leadership Development Program, which is Compassion's other main program. After sponsored kids graduate from high school, they have the opportunity to be sponsored through college. There is a very stringent selection process. Since the ultimate aim is to raise up Christian leaders, the applicants have to be professing Christians, have outstanding grades and show definite leadership potential. The kids we met on this night were nothing short of magnificent and inspiring as they shared some of their stories with us.

We said goodbye and the thoughts of every team member turned to the next few hours when we would meet our sponsored children...

Philippines Day 6-Child-sponsor Visit Day
Friday 12 April 2013
So finally, Friday came around. If we were all honest, the moment the twelve people who came on this trip were anticipating the most was this day. It was the long-awaited sponsor-child visit day here in the

Philippines. This week, I and 13 other adventurous Australians have witnessed incredible and heartbreaking stuff. Such joy, love, gratitude and generosity in the midst of circumstances we can't even imagine. We talked with mums and dads, and visited the places they call home. We played and sang songs with kids and babies. We witnessed the difference that God and Compassion are making in the lives of so many people.

However, today it got personal. We welcomed our 12 sponsored children (three of them were mine) plus one parent and Project worker to Manila for a day of fun at Manila Ocean Park and Jollibee's restaurant. For most, if not all, the kids it was their first time on a plane and their first time in Manila. It was like another universe for them.

As many Compassion sponsor visits as I have done, I have to say it never gets old, predictable or boring. There are always certain feelings and emotions that are ever-present. There is the anticipation and excitement of seeing these kids face-to-face. Finally the investment of letters, money, encouragement, love and prayer will pay off in a meeting where I can hold, talk to and interact with this precious life that God has entrusted to me. There is the anxiety of how they'll respond to me: *will they be affectionate or give me nothing at all?* (I've had both extremes) *How will the language barrier affect our interaction? Will I remember everything I planned to say?* Sometimes even the best-intentioned list of questions goes out the window when you see their home environment and learn more about their circumstances.

For me, this visit was going to be monumentally different to anything I had experienced previously. There would be no visiting their home environment, community, house or Project, which are the places they feel some sort of comfort and familiarity. By flying my three kids to Manila I was essentially uprooting them from everything they had ever known. Culture shock on a major scale.

As good as today was, for me it was another occasion God had to teach me a lesson. One that I have had to learn repeatedly. Sometimes things don't go the way I want them to and sometimes my expectations will not be met. Mine weren't today. But for crying out loud, it's not about me. The kids were experiencing a day where their dreams were coming true, or even beyond that. My oldest Princess Joy said she didn't even imagine that I would come to visit. It wasn't even in her sphere of imagination or dreaming. That's how significant a sponsor visit is.

For me, today was about Cashofia (7), John Dave (8) and Princess Joy (12). The younger two didn't cope well on the bus, but once we arrived they were yapping away and warmed to me immediately. I had one sweaty little hand on either side of me the whole time. I gave them a soft toy kangaroo at the start as an ice-breaker and they took them everywhere for the whole day.

We visited the Oceanarium, the sea-lion show and went on a small glass-bottomed boat looking at sea creatures. Things seemed rushed and we didn't really get the chance to enjoy each other, talk to or play with each other much. Lunch was at Jollibee's restaurant, with spaghetti and rice replacing the usual burger and chips. I was the 'centerpiece' on our table of ten, eight of whom were female. Miraculously, I managed not to spill any of the spaghetti, which is my least favorite food in terms of eating in public. I also got to strut my stuff by teaching the whole group our 'theme song' for the week, Baking a Cake.

The end came far too soon, though not for my two youngest, who fell asleep on the bus. Our gift-giving, final conversations and family prayers had to be done on the bus, which was not ideal and made things seemed rushed but the few minutes I had with each mother and child were still special. I never got the opportunity to talk with the mothers in any sort of detail about the positives and challenges they face in their home lives.

In our final minutes I took each mother, child and Project worker/translator up the front of the bus and this was their final opportunity to ask any questions or share anything they wanted me to know, or wanted prayer for. I encouraged them to be honest.

Two of them didn't give much away but one of the mothers broke down as she shared about a situation with her husband. They are still together, but he has been accused of committing a terrible crime against one of his employees and has been forced into hiding due to the sworn vengeance of the alleged victim's family. His wife knows where he is and is in contact with him by phone. She and the three children have not seen their husband and father for three years. He is obviously missed, but maybe God has me in there in the meantime as a 'stand-in' father? Who knows? I appreciated her honesty and the trust she showed by telling me that story.

Once again, being able to pray with and for the families was humbling and a privilege. These kids have a hard life but because of Compassion they have dreams (I have two future teachers and a policeman) and a realistic opportunity to achieve them.

One thing I appreciated about being on a group tour, as opposed to an individual trip, was the chance to hear stories about the other sponsors relationships with their sponsored children. One couple were meeting the 18-year-old girl they had sponsored for 12 years. It was heartbreakingly precious to see the photos of them together on this special day. On this trip they discovered just how significant the letters are to the kids and pledged to write more often. Another couple had been blessed to visit their child's home the previous week and met her again on the child-sponsor visit day.

There were stories of hardship and sacrifice among my fellow sponsors on their journey to visit their sponsored kids, but on this day there was also an overwhelming sense of peace and joy that our God had orchestrated this trip from the very start, details were His specialty and this day of meeting face-to-face was His reward.

Journey #5—Colombia, Ecuador, Peru, September 2013

Visiting Laura in Colombia

Monday 23 September 2013

My latest Compassion adventure began with 33 hours of travel and four flights. Definitely the scenic route. Destination: Bogota, Colombia. I arrived in Bogota at 5.00am and my translator Leonardo was good enough to meet me at the airport straight away. It just meant we had a few hours to kill. We chatted and he told me a bit of his story. Colombia is known as a predominantly Catholic country. His sister was the first in their family to become a Christian at age 16 and as a result she was kicked out of home. He has been working with Compassion for a while and at one stage was translating letters.

At first he translated the sponsor letters from English to Spanish. He noted the common theme of the letters: God loves you and has a plan for you despite the poverty and despite your circumstances. Jeremiah 29:11 came up a lot. He admitted at first he had a certain amount of skepticism, along the lines of "*Yeah they're rich and they have 'stuff', of course they're going to say God is good.*"

But things changed when he started translating the kid's letters. They would share with their sponsors the hard things that were happening in their lives, but then would add "*but it doesn't matter because I have Jesus in my life and He will take care of me and my family.*" This impacted Leonardo immeasurably and, like the majority of Compassion translators I've been privileged to meet, he is a passionate advocate for Compassion and the fight against poverty. He helped make my day a joyful experience.

I have been sponsoring Laura for over two years. She is about to turn 14 and of course is the same height as me. Laura writes fantastic detailed letters and had expressed in a few of them the desire to meet me. It really is a dream that all sponsored kids have. Never doubt that, and if you get the opportunity to go on a trip, GO!

Laura's family consists of Mama, older brother Alejandro (15) and younger sister Mariana (5). They have no father or husband living at home and I heard mention of at least two different fathers. I was happy to learn that one of them still helps the family with money, since Mama does not work because she has to care for her youngest child. This has left Alejandro as the man of the house. I have wondered how this would weigh on the heart of a 15-year-old boy, whether the expectations were explicit or left unsaid. During our day together he appeared to be a bright, enthusiastic, animated young fella, and it was a pleasure to meet him.

To meet Laura and her family we ventured down to South Bogota, which has its share of challenges. Even taxi drivers are hesitant to go there. I have no pictures of the neighborhood because it's not safe. Robberies and teenage gangs are a major problem.

The school system in Colombia operates in two sessions: 6am–12pm, then 1pm–6pm. A major reason there are so many problems with the young people is that when they get out of school, they have nowhere to go and nothing to do. Many families are fractured and the parent is working all day, so the kids stay out on the street.

Traveling in a taxi on the way to lunch we stopped at a red light and very nearly witnessed a 'schoolyard street rumble.' Boys in school uniforms were baiting each other with words and their weapons of choice were planks of wood that would do a bit of damage. Some of them started throwing wood onto the nature strip in the middle of the road, very close to our taxi. Something was said that tipped them over the edge and boys scattered in all directions, some chasing and some fleeing. Then the light turned green.

The Project Laura and Alejandro attend has been operating for nine years. There were no activities on this day so I took a tour and met the staff. Heroes of mine.

148

They started with 150 kids and have grown to 350. Here's the thing: the church that the Project is attached to only has about 70 members. *A church of 70 looking after and caring for 350 kids in a dangerous gang-ridden community?* It's stories like that that make me so convinced that Compassion is a God-thing. And funnily enough, the Compassion Project workers get left alone by the gangs.

I learned that the Project were beneficiaries of Compassion's Complementary Interventions program (CIV), where if a Project has a specific pressing need, such as more toilets or a better quality kitchen, they can apply for funding from Compassion. This Project was able to build themselves a new kitchen thanks to the CIV.

One of the things I love seeing at every Project I visit is the cupboards full of child folders that detail and document every area of a child's development–school progress, medical reports, social development and sponsor correspondence. Everything that is sent and received-gifts, money, letters, is recorded. The integrity and accountability is outstanding.

We visited Laura's home where we met the rest of the family. They have been living there for ten years. Their house belonged to Laura's grandfather, who had been killed just two months before in a robbery gone wrong. He was the only breadwinner, so his death put a massive strain on the family. Thankfully (and unsurprisingly) Compassion stepped up to help, and they also get help from Mama's sister and one of the kid's fathers.

It's times like that when I fully grasp the significance and impact of a sponsor. God is using me to literally be a father to the fatherless, to give Laura words of love and encouragement, which she doesn't necessarily get from anywhere else.

While at the house, I gave out some gifts. For each child on this trip I gave an activity book, colored pencils, a sharpener, bubbles, a soft toy kangaroo or koala and a 'Where's Wally?' book. The family received a 2014 calendar with images of Australia.

Laura and Alejandro both attend a unique school which is half an hour out of town. I learned that it is a normal public school, but because it is rural they are able to do things like plant crops and grow gardens. This gives the kids invaluable income-generating skills for their futures. On the flip-side, because of the distance and the fact school starts at 6am, they are up at 4am and out the door an hour later. Tough for a couple of young teens.

I was told that the bus route had been changed because on one occasion Laura, Alejandro and the kids they were with were robbed on their way to the bus stop. The thieves took everything including their shoes, and they had to walk home shoeless and crying.

One reason I'm so passionate about sponsors visiting their kids if they ever get the slightest opportunity, apart from the fact that it's their biggest dream, is that you find out so much that you otherwise wouldn't know just from the letters. Now, this can be a good or bad thing, depending on the family's circumstances. When I went to Central America in January there were plenty of things about the kid's home situations that I would rather have not known. But I know that if I am to love them like God loves them, I have to put my heart out there and risk getting hurt. I can't pretend that injustice and horrible circumstances don't exist. I can't hide from it.

For lunch we headed out to a mall. Laura was indecisive about choosing a venue in the food court. I didn't take my chance to choose when offered either, so bizarrely we settled on this Chinese rice/noodle place. I was still dealing with stomach issues so I wasn't very hungry, and then found a mountain of food placed in front of me. Let's just say the family took home a rather large doggy bag. You're welcome.

A classic moment came when it was time to go on the escalator to go to the next level at the mall. Mama just would not go on, no matter how much we cajoled or encouraged her–it was a legitimate phobia. She even nearly sent me tumbling down on one occasion when I had her by the hand and was about to go on and she pulled back at the last second. She was quite happy to take the stairs.

After lunch we went to an amusement arcade located in the mall. The kids had a blast (oh, what the heck, so did I). They tried all sorts of games and attractions but the clear favorite was the Bumper Cars. Not surprisingly I was the main target but I gave as good as I got. We had about four goes and I escaped generally unscathed, although I'm pretty sure I heard something crack at one point.

Air hockey was also popular. I played against both Laura and Alejandro and as much as I wanted to, I just couldn't let them beat me. After hearing many of the details of the lives of this family and the challenges they face, it was a gift from God to be able to give them a couple of hours of fun, just being kids.

After a fantastic day it was time for me to go. I thought long and hard about what I was going to say to them at the end. What words could I leave with them? I settled on this:

> *After our day together, I'm sure you have an idea of how much I love you. But as much as I love you, I need you to know that God loves you so much more. He has given me just a little taste of His love for you. I pray that you continue to trust in Him and look to Him for all your needs.*

Re-visiting Jacqueline in Ecuador
Tuesday 24 September 2013
What I saw and experienced during my Central America trip in January absolutely wrecked my heart and spirit. I believe God was trying to give me a glimpse of what he sees every day, but then He also showed me the hope in the form of Compassion and the impact they are having on children and families.

My third-last visit on this trip was to Ecuador, where I met 6-year-old Jacqueline. Looking back on that day I see God's mercy. I think He thought

I'd seen enough hard stuff and gave me a day of complete and pure joy. We went to an amusement park and she just had the time of her life. On this day she conked out after lunch and fell asleep in my arms on the ride home. It was an incredibly profound moment for me. I am not a father yet but that day I felt the love of a father for his child. I reflected later that God was teaching me about trust and the way a child trusts when they fall asleep in your arms is the way He wants people to trust Him.

When I was planning the trip for September 2013, Brazil was definitely in, and Colombia and Peru were definitely in because I hadn't visited the two kids in those countries. Then I thought *"How can I go back to South America and not go to Ecuador again?"* So, nine months after the first visit, I was back.

Jacqui lives with her parents and is one of five children. Her oldest sister is twenty and has a son and a daughter, so Jacqui is a 'tia' (aunt) at six. She also has a twin brother and two other older sisters. I didn't get to meet her father last time, since he was working as a security guard at a mall. Mama makes and sells leggings and pants. She has a little workshop set up in their home. It is one of the nicer homes I have seen in my visits to my sponsored kids.

When I arrived at the Compassion Ecuador office, the first thing I did was catch up on things since our last visit. They had been facing eviction from their rented house but thankfully they had been able to negotiate a deal with the landlord, and so were still there. I asked about their pet rabbit, unfortunately it died after falling down the steep steps in their house. However, now they had a little black puppy. I asked about the father's job. He chose to leave his security job since he had to work too much and didn't get to see his family as often as he would like. He was now washing cars at the mall with his brother.

Jacqueline is only in first grade but she is already facing enormous challenges in her schoolwork. She struggles in most areas and this is only compounded by the fact her twin brother is very bright and finds it all easy. She was actually facing exams later in the week to see if she will pass to second grade.

We went to Volcano Park, the same amusement park as the previous visit. I am very fortunate not to suffer from altitude sickness, as we were a *long* way up. Since today was Tuesday, a normal school/work day (Jacqui had been given the day off school), the place was empty and we actually arrived 45 minutes before it opened, so we had some time to kill.

Jacqui is one of the most outgoing, animated and affectionate little people I know. She 'took me to school' in the art of two-way conversation. She would talk for five minutes straight then handball it over to me with a *"Now it's your turn. What would you like to say?"* She even threw in that question that she will learn is pretty useless to ask a man: *"What are you thinking about right now?"*

We talked about anything and everything, and I sang some songs with her, which I naughtily forgot to do last time. I got the Australian football out and we had a bit of throw and catch as well as races in the vacant car park.

Before we knew it, the park was open and it was rides, slides, trampolines and sideshows galore. I went on with her when I was allowed to and once again was caught up in the pure innocence and joy of being a child. I had brought her a large Dora the Explorer soft toy (a gift from one of my students) and it was literally half her size. We played on of those whack-a-mole games and I won her another little soft toy. She was happy to have a friend for Dora.

Lunch was KFC at a local mall which just happened to be the mall where her father works, washing cars with his brother. He travels over an hour each way, six days a week. It was great to be able to meet him. We had a short, friendly conversation based on what I knew about him already and I encouraged him for working hard to provide for his family, which now consists of five kids and two grandchildren. God has provided for them in that both parents are able to work and then throw in Compassion for that bit of extra help. Three of the five children are sponsored.

We then went to visit their house again, where all the siblings (and the little black puppy) were waiting for us. Jacqui's twin brother is an absolute circus. He was non-stop and his little niece and nephew were toddling around following him everywhere. In between that and the puppy running around licking faces, I was able to have a good conversation with Mama and the older sisters.

Mama is struggling to juggle everything involved with trying to work and raise five kids and two grandkids, but her faith in God is strong and sure and she is so grateful for the extra help Compassion provides, particularly in regard to school supplies. I learned that Tuesday and Saturday are the days she sells the pants and leggings she makes but she had taken this day off in order to be with me and allow Jacqui to have her special day.

There's something humbling about the sacrifice of the poor. God is doing great things in this family and He has given me a front row seat.

Visiting Cristina in Peru
Wednesday 25 September 2013
On Wednesday, the third stop on my Compassion adventure was Peru, where I sponsor 10-year-old Cristina. She was one of two remaining sponsored kids I had not visited.

Initially Lima turned on quite a grey, cold and wet day, though it warmed up later. We headed down to the very south of Lima. The drive to the Project was interesting. The environment was rather drab, dusty and colorless, with severely underdeveloped roads and buildings, and cacti growing in the median strips. I imagine it would be a challenge for many people to maintain any sort of hopes or dreams as they eked out an existence in that environment.

On the way I sensed that God was going to teach me something on this day, and I was right. It wasn't one of those overly joyous 'made-in-heaven' type of days that we all hope for when we meet our sponsored kids, but I guess not all of them can be, and I've had my fair share anyway.

Cristina turned 10 on Monday, she found out the next day I was coming and I was there on the Wednesday. What an amazing birthday present! We met at the Project and she was quiet and cautious. I was taken on a tour, took some photos and saw Cristina's classroom. There were no Project activities at this time because the kids were at school, so we came back later in the day.

A highlight from the Project was the 'Sponsor Wall' in each classroom. This is where they list the names of each child and their sponsor, then once a week they have a special time where they pray for all the sponsors. I know I certainly feel it at times-the sense of God's supernatural peace and blessing even when life seems normal or boring. It is because I have kids, parents and Project workers praying for me.

After a while we visited Cristina's home, where we met Mama and her older brother Enrique. Her younger sister was at school and her father was working. The house has been given to them by one of Cristina's grandparents and they've been living there for 14 years. It is small and cramped but they have a bathroom with a toilet and electricity.

There was also a fridge and a washing machine. This is not because they are well-off, and they are still paying them off, but because they participate in a special arrangement with three or four other families which I understand is quite common in Peru. Every month, one of the families receives an agreed-upon amount of money from the rest of the families which enables them to purchase necessary supplies or appliances. The next month it's a different family's turn to receive the money.

Both Cristina's parents work. Mama makes a special fruit-based dessert and sells it at a local market. Her dad is a freelance soccer coach/trainer who coaches teams or individuals according to demand. It is not stable or secure work but on this day he was working. He is 46 years old but apparently he was the equivalent of a state-level soccer player in Peru back in the day.

I gave Cristina some gifts with a couple of extra soft toys thrown in because it was her birthday (and also to lighten the suitcase). She received them with quiet gratitude.

After this we went to a local mall for lunch and I observed Cristina as we walked past all sorts of shops. She soaked in the noise, the atmosphere and the busyness, and I got the sense it was like a different universe to her. We had chicken and chips for lunch and for some reason I agreed to order a salad bowl. It was here I discovered Cristina's absolute dislike for anything that looks even remotely like salad. Mama and I proceeded to light-heartedly try and get her to have some salad and they took the uneaten food home in a bag. I said jokingly *"So is that your dinner for the next week?"* I don't think she saw the funny side.

Mama was pleasant, friendly and good to talk to. She and the kids are committed Christians and involved in their church, the brother only more recently. He could be a key player in getting their father along. Cristina's father is staunch Catholic and that's the excuse he has always used for avoiding church. I have the feeling that eventually, when he sees the changes in his kids and the love of the Compassion staff for his family, who knows what will happen down the track? Continuing to pray…

It was during this time and on the drive back to the Project that I discovered sometimes not even a sponsor visiting from the other side of the world can interrupt a strong mother-daughter bond. With her mother, Cristina was a different child. She laughed, smiled, babbled away and was so much more relaxed. It was good to see that side of her, even if I wasn't the cause of it.

David Chalmers

At the Project in the afternoon I was able to meet Cristina's friends and classmates. The weather had warmed up as we played and sang and had a great time. There is no language barrier when it comes to having fun with kids.

I left Cristina with some words, encouraging her to always work hard and try her best because that's all God expects us to do. I prayed God would show her what she is good at and what she loves to do, and she would be able to spend her life doing that, bringing glory to Him.

The main lesson I learned from today is that true and genuine love gives generously, extravagantly and lavishly without expecting anything in return. The ultimate example of this, of course, is Jesus coming from heaven as a man in order to make us right with God. His death and resurrection paid the price for us, and we can be seen as righteous in God's sight. There is nothing we can do to earn or deserve this. It is a gift of mercy and grace from God.

In my own small way, I hoped today I was following Jesus' example of genuine, extravagant, sacrificial love, and I know Cristina appreciated it even if she didn't show it physically. Thank you God for the opportunity.

Journey #6 – Philippines 2014

In 2014, obeying what I believed to be the call of God, I left everything in Australia behind and went to work in an orphanage in the Philippines called **The Ruel Foundation**. What I saw and experienced on my various Compassion journeys really impacted me, and each time I came back to Australia I struggled adjusting and settling in to our culture. Such affluence, abundance and prosperity, yet we can be so greedy, prideful, self-sufficient and ungrateful for what we have. I carried an increasing sense of discomfort and discontent, along with a feeling that I may be called to serve God in faraway lands.

As I was going to be a volunteer I was no longer able to financially sponsor my Compassion kids. In November 2013 I put the word out and I kid you not, within a month all my kids were sponsored by my generous family and friends, many of them encountering Compassion for the first time. God used the passionate heart He has given me to inspire others to live generously and sacrificially.

I loved many things about Philippines life. The weather was magnificent. Driving a tricycle was always an adventure. The cost of living was incredibly cheap. My workload was anything but demanding, teaching a class of five students for half-days. I used the Facebook page and the blog to increase people's knowledge of Ruel and the work they do. I was able to give people opportunities to help and be part of God's work in caring for orphaned and abandoned little ones.

It didn't end up being the long-term experience I thought it might be. The constant struggles and challenges I faced in terms of adapting to the culture and building relationships proved too much for me. I also missed being a hands-on uncle to my five nieces and nephews, as well as my involvement with Compassion as a sponsor and advocate.

During the year, I made the decision to visit my three former sponsored kids in the Philippines in late September/early October. They all had new sponsors: **Cashofia** was sponsored by my friends Clarisse and Paul; **John Dave** was sponsored by my parents and **Princess Joy** was sponsored by my friend Dani. It was extra special to be able to visit on their behalf and give them a glimpse into their child's life that very few sponsors get. Part of the reason for this trip was that when we met in Manila in April 2013 I wasn't able to visit their homes and communities, which is what I really wanted to experience.

So the nine-day trip was organized for September 25 to October 3. True to form, it was anything but a relaxing "do-nothing getaway," since when I travel I have to have a meaningful purpose or goal. I would be visiting the three kids, as well as meeting some American missionaries for the first time and catching up with some Compassion friends.

This trip was only my second time off the island of Oriental Mindoro in the eight months I had been living in the Philippines. Right from the start I saw God at work, providing friends along the way to help me out. On the ferry I sat next to a man who I learned was named Ian. We got talking and I told him all about Ruel and why I was in the Philippines. He also told me all about his life and ministry. After we got off the ferry Ian helped me navigate through the maze of taxi guys trying to rip me off and got me safely on a van.

My first stop was an orphanage called *Mercy House of the Philippines* in Silang, Cavite. It is relatively new and is run by an American called Nikki and her Filipino husband Anthony. They are involved in rescuing and restoring street kids and are motivated purely by God's love. We connected through Facebook and it was great to meet them in person. Nikki and Anthony have two biological children, five adopted Filipino boys and eight other kids being cared for through Mercy House. They all live together in a nice two-story building and are currently seeking God's direction in terms of expansion.

I arrived mid-afternoon on Thursday after a two-hour crowded van ride in which my knees were squashed and I could hardly move. Not good for the arthritis, but there wasn't much I could do about it. I met the staff and kids, had dinner with them and the kids then put on a singing and dancing show. The next morning I went with them to the market and they generously dropped me off at the airport in Manila for my flight to Davao.

One thing I realized from travelling to a different city is how 'normal' poverty had become to me. I had been in Calapan City for eight months and I had become used to the shocking conditions many people live in on a daily basis. It no longer impacted me the way it did when I travelled from Australia to the developing world. However, I was hit again when we were driving through Silang, past squatter communities on the side of the road literally being bulldozed to the ground, leaving real people displaced with nowhere to go. All it took was a change of scenery to wake me up again.

I made it to my Davao flight, and we sat on the tarmac for 40 minutes before finally taking off. We arrived in Davao in darkness and pouring rain and I was met by my friend Maricel, who agreed to pick me up from the airport. She got me safely to my hotel, and then we headed to SM Lanang mall to meet with a couple of other Compassion friends, Michelle Tolentino (whose story I have shared earlier in the book) as well as Rafonzel, who I met for the first time. I had seen an amazing video of Rafonzel meeting her Australian sponsor for the first time on stage at a conference, and it was great to meet her in person.

When we met it was late, and nothing was open except an expensive coffee shop. I hadn't eaten since lunchtime, I so scarfed down a muffin and a shake. I felt bad being the only one eating, but they were very gracious about it. Michelle and Rafonzel were in the middle of a busy week of planning a conference for her ministry Made In Hope. We had an enjoyable conversation for about an hour, and I appreciated them giving their time to me.

Visiting Cashofia in Davao
Saturday 27 September, 2014
I was picked up from my hotel by Pastor Rick, Project Director of PH521, Davao Shekinah Child Development Center. We travelled by taxi to the community of Mandug, which I was told used to be a banana plantation,

but it was pulled down amid riots caused by the fact that chemicals were being used, and people weren't happy with this.

The Project is relatively new. It has been running for four years and has 160 kids. As a result, the oldest kids are only 10 and 11 years old. We arrived at the Project to a raucous bunch of joyful kids singing and dancing during their morning devotion time. They were wearing different colored shirts according to their age group. This was the first time I had seen this at a Project.

I was introduced and met with smiles and curiosity. Part of their devotion time was celebrating children who had birthdays. I mentioned that my birthday was in four days and they hastily adjusted the Powerpoint screen and put my name up there. They also sang to me, and I was asked to pray for the birthday kids. I felt very welcomed and 'at home' straight away.

Next I was taken to meet the Project office staff, who work behind the scenes to make sure everything about the Project is done with excellence and integrity. They showed me Cashofia's folder and all the letters I had sent her. It was quite a thick pile. I was also taken on a tour of the Project and had photos taken with each class of kids. During this time I was approached by many of the kids and we interacted with smiles, high-fives and a funny finger trick.

At the Compassion Projects, groups of children are assigned a caseworker who follows up concerns with the families, takes care of appointments and many other things. I was introduced to Cashofia's caseworker, a beautiful young woman named Cely. Pastor Rick told me the story of how they met. He was at a mall, and Cely asked to borrow his cellphone. They got talking and she mentioned she wanted to work in children's ministry. It just so happened that Cashofia's previous caseworker had just finished up, so he was able to interview her and offer her a job. The best part is that **Cely is a former sponsored child as well**, so she is able to offer the children a living example of God's love and what the future can be like for them because of Compassion.

After having a wonderful time at the Project, we travelled by motorized tricycle to Cashofia's house. Home visits are always the most challenging part of the day for me, but I like to see the children in their natural environment, where they are most comfortable.

Cashofia is now nine years old and in Grade 4 at school, which is right nearby. I met her mother (who I had already met in Manila in 2013), her 13-year-old sister Rachel and her seven-year-old brother Jomari. I found out that Rachel shares my birthday, and was turning 13. Mama teaches a Values class at Cashofia's school and sells meat during the day. Her husband does not live with them due to some unfortunate circumstances which will not be resolved any time soon. I found this out last year, and I knew it was risky to bring it up again. Both Mama and Cashofia started crying as soon as I mentioned him; they miss him very much. He works in a different area and sends money to support them.

The family's house is right by a river, so they have it elevated a couple of meters off the ground. It kind of reminded me of a treehouse. It has three rooms and is made entirely of wood. The front room is completely open, with no privacy, windows or curtains. I foolishly asked "*What happens when it rains?*" The reply was matter-of-fact: "*We get wet.*" They have one bedroom where all four family members sleep together on the wooden floor, no mattress, no pillows. They have to buy their water for washing, cooking and drinking, and have no bathroom facilities. They use Mama's sister's house, which is just next door.

Just like any family they are proud of their achievements, so medals and certificates are displayed on the wall in the front room. The family was very friendly and easy to engage, so we had a really enjoyable conversation. They showed me some photos of Cashofia and I showed some photos of my life at Ruel and also a couple of family photos of her new sponsors Paul and Clarisse McGregor. I think the family enjoyed the fact that Clarisse is a Filipina, and their three children look similar to them. I also gave Cashofia some gifts I had bought the night before: a puzzle, a coloring book, a game of Bingo and Snakes and Ladders. Her eyes positively lit up when she saw me reach into my bag.

A significant moment of the day came when we met Cashofia's grandmother. She is 49, though she looks a lot older, and had been paralyzed for a few weeks after a work accident. I was asked to pray for her, which is something I don't take lightly. I was not able to put my hands on her spine, since she was on her back and could not move, so I put my hands on her head and we spent the next 15 minutes just praying. It was incredibly profound. The Pastor and the other staff who came along joined in with me as we called on the power of God to bring healing in the name of Jesus. We knew that such a miracle would do wonders for bringing hope to that community.

There was no instant cure, and we knew that no matter how much begging, pleading, beseeching or proclaiming we did, ultimately it's up to God as to when, how and even 'if' He heals her. It's hard walking away from something like that with no immediate visible results, but it's a challenging exercise in faith and trust, believing that the One who is mighty to save and heal will do it. I will continue to pray for her, and look forward to the day that healing comes.

We walked to Cashofia's school which was just nearby, saw her classroom and met some of the teachers. Then we travelled back to the Project for a delicious lunch with all the Project staff.

After lunch we went to a local hotel called the Waterfront Hotel. It was exquisite, with incredible views and amazing facilities. Pastor Rick used to work there many years ago, and still thinks it's the best hotel in Davao. We took some family photos and went for a walk around the grounds.

Next stop was the SM Lanang mall for some games and ice cream. We travelled by jeepney, which was one of six modes of transport I experienced on this day. It was a great way to spend $7.50, and the kids had lots of fun in the arcade, with the basketball game a particularly big hit.

For me, our last activity of the day was the most amazing. So simple and so taken for granted in our part of the world, but on this day the supermarket at Gaisano mall was the scene of a big adventure. Cashofia's sponsors, the McGregors, had sent a monetary gift for the family to spend on whatever they needed (and trust me, there's a lot of things they need). So the family, Pastor Rick, Cely and I loaded up a shopping cart and went on a 'grocery adventure' around the packed supermarket FOR THE FIRST TIME EVER!

There are no words to adequately describe the looks of excitement on the faces of the kids as we traipsed the aisles, dodged countless other shoppers, accidently rammed people with the shopping cart and they were able to choose special treat items for themselves. To me, it was a pure example of the Love of God in action. People who have been given much were giving to those with less, supplying their needs and, as an added bonus, giving them a memory that will last a long time. Because of Compassion and Cashofia's sponsor, this family knows that God loves them enough to provide someone to help them with their basic needs.

Loaded up with several heavy bags full of goodies and enough rice to last them quite a while, the family took a taxi home, ending an amazing visit day. I have to say that no matter how many child visit days I do, it never gets old or any less impacting. The impact that Compassion, the church and sponsors have on these children and families is simply immeasurable, and to be part of it is the greatest way I can spend my life.

My day ended with a visit to another couple of US missionaries, Daniel and Marlene Bray. We connected firstly through Marlene's blog and then via Facebook. Back in November 2013 she wrote a blog post that for some reason went a bit crazy on the internet nine months later. It was entitled "*20 Things No-One Tells You About Moving Overseas.*" For me it was literally a God-sent piece of prose, since I read it just as I was starting to enter the 'frustration' stage of culture shock and it gave me some perspective about what I was dealing with.

The Brays have a ministry to street kids in Davao called 'Hope Created', and Daniel also teaches at a local school. They have two children; their son Andrew is living with them but their daughter is going to college back in the US.

When I knew I was coming to Davao, we got in contact and arranged to meet. On this night we went out for some Indian food. I've never been a fan of spicy stuff, but we found a couple of dishes that were very mild and I was all sorted. We had an enjoyable few hours together, and I was able to share about the work of Ruel Foundation and talk through some of my culture shock stuff. I was really grateful to be able to talk to some people who 'get it', and blessed to have some new friends.

Visiting John Dave in Canlaon City
Monday 29 September, 2014
The next stop on my journey was John Dave in Canlaon City, who is now sponsored by my parents. To get to John Dave's home required a long bus trip. I arrived in Bacolod about 5.30pm, and as the shuttle bus was driving to the bus terminal, the passengers all agreed that there would be no more buses that night. The driver seized this business opportunity and offered to take me there directly, for a relatively exorbitant fee. I didn't really have much choice, so away we went.

The driver was a friendly old chap called Vincent. He asked me why I was in Bacolod and I was able to share with him about my work with Ruel and Compassion. By this time it was dark, and after all the other passengers were dropped off he pulled over and transferred me to his brother's van, *"because my eyesight isn't very strong,"* he said as he squinted at me from close range. I believed him.

Well, the next three-and-a-half hours were a crazy adventure. I give him credit for trying to get me there in record time, but you have to drive to the conditions. The roads were atrociously bumpy and pot-holey but he rarely slowed down, resulting in a long trip of bumps and jolts that wasn't much fun. Like I thought he might, the driver tried to wrangle a few extra hundred pesos out of me when we arrived in Canlaon City, but I wasn't having any of that. Because I hadn't eaten since lunchtime, the first thing I did was wolf down a cheeseburger and a club sandwich, and went to bed relieved, content and on a full stomach.

In the morning I was picked up by Crystal, the Project Director of PH813, Lampara Child Development Center, where John Dave attends. The Project has been running for 24 years, and currently has 373 kids of all ages in their sponsorship program. They also have 41 mothers and babies in their Child Survival Program, which is funded by a couple from Tasmania.

This day was not an activity day, but all the staff were there. When we arrived I was greeted with smiles and met John Dave's whole family. His Mum works for the government on short term contracts. His Dad is a bodyguard for the city Mayor. He normally works every day but had taken this day off to see me. There are four children in the family: Jeannel is 15 and in 9th Grade. She didn't seem too sure what she wanted to do once she left school, but she came up with 'nurse.' Bryan is 14 and he wants to be a soccer player. Robin is 12 and he wants to be a scientist. John Dave is nine and he wants to be a doctor. The older three speak and understand some English, so it made communicating a lot easier and more enjoyable.

We had a short conversation with the family, then I was introduced to all the staff in a barrage of names, and taken on a tour of the Project. When we got to the church John Dave was keen to show me his drumming skills. He was very good for a little guy, and learns to play as part of Project activities. Of course I got on the drums straight after, and all the staff joined in a drums-only version of 'One Way, Jesus.'

I have to say, in my experience the friendliest Filipinos seem to be the ones who are associated with Compassion. This group of staff were incredibly welcoming and joyful, and they came with us everywhere during the day, so there was always a nice convoy of motorcycles following our truck. Normally it's just the translator and Project Director who accompany me. The best thing is, about seven of the staff are former sponsored children themselves, including the Project Director!

The home visit was next. The family had been living in their current house for about three years and they own the rights to it, which means they don't have to pay anything to stay there. The house has three rooms: living room, one bedroom for the parents and one bedroom for all four kids (poor 15 year old Jeannel!). They sleep at the back of the house, and one of the walls was destroyed by a falling tree during a typhoon, and still hadn't been repaired. They put a big mattress up against the wall in an attempt to keep out the cold and rain.

Early on in the day John Dave had been subdued and visibly distressed due to a persistent toothache. I was really worried this was going to affect our day together or even cut it short. When I prayed for the family at their house, I asked God for healing for John Dave. I closely studied him for the rest of the day and there was not a single time he put his hand to his mouth or showed signs of discomfort. God is a healer!

The next stop was lunch at my hotel for the whole family and the Project staff. I met the senior Pastor of the church, Pastor Bert and we chatted. After this we jumped in the back of our truck and headed on a nice, bumpy, uphill ride to see the "Century Tree," which is about 400 years old. I had never seen anything like it, it was just mammoth. I believe it is a sacred site, and we had to stop into the tourism office to ask permission to go there. I was told it used to be the location for spirit worship and people were afraid to go there because of superstition and fear of the beings that were living in the tree.

While there, we were able to have a kick of the Australian football, or as John Dave called it, "the red ostrich egg." I met John Dave back in April 2013, but he had to share me with my two other sponsored kids. I got the sense that today he enjoyed having me to himself. He was very animated and fascinated with me. My white and hairy arms and legs were the focus of constant attention, he would rub them slowly with a sense of wonder. It was funny to watch.

The final task for the day was shopping. Canlaon is a small town and doesn't have a mall, so we went to the market in the middle of town. I gave Mama some money to buy the family groceries, and I gave each of the kids the equivalent of $10 to buy whatever they wanted. I could tell by their reaction that they had rarely, if ever, been entrusted with that amount of money before, and it was humbling to see their sense of anticipation as we walked to the shops. The older three kids bought some shoes and there were also badminton racquets, a basketball, a SpongeBob Squarepants backpack and a Ben10 video game.

Finally it was time to go. The whole crew followed us to the bus terminal, the guys grabbed my bags and plonked me safely in the front seat of the big coach headed for Bacolod. They worded up the driver about who I was and where I was going and waved me off when the bus left. I was so grateful to be so well looked after and cared for. I praise God for the staff at Project PH813 and I know He will continue to bless them.

Visiting Princess Joy
Wednesday 1 October, 2014
Once again, another big travel day was required in order to visit Princess Joy. Tuesday involved two flights and a long bus trip (that sounds familiar). The flights were fine, and at 4.00pm I arrived in Tacloban, which was at the center of one of the big typhoons in 2013.

The baggage guy took me to an unmarked taxi. I knew I should have refused, since they always charge more than the metered taxis, but I was tired so I just went with him. God was about to teach me another lesson. The driver quoted his price, which indeed was relatively steep. I was initially annoyed, but my attitude soon changed. He told me I was his first passenger for the day (at 4pm!), he lost his house in the typhoon and he has four kids at home. He told me about the high price of food and the conditions they live in.

I initially held on to my skepticism. Indeed, he could have been making some of it up for sympathy, but as he was talking I was looking out the window and the scene was still one of destruction and devastation, even months later. Little tin shacks were their 'houses', people were wandering around aimlessly, selling anything they could to get enough for food. The level of poverty I saw actually reminded of what I saw in Haiti when I visited in 2013, and is not something I will forget easily. No one here had a 'sob story', they were genuinely and legitimately suffering, nearly a year after the typhoon hit.

The driver got me to the bus terminal safely and I handed over his fare, with a different attitude than when we first met. The transport this time was not a great big comfy coach, but a little 14-seater van, and I found myself squashed between my luggage and a big lady in the back row. Most of the journey was completed in that eerie atmosphere created when there are sheets of lightning but no thunder or rain. About halfway through the trip we got a flat tyre, then of course it started to rain.

The trip ended up taking over five hours, and we arrived at the terminal at 10.45pm. A small mercy occurred when I asked the tricycle driver where my hotel was, and he pointed across the road! We had literally landed right across the road from my hotel, for which I was exceedingly thankful. I hit the hay pretty much straight away. I was ready and excited for the final child visit, Princess Joy on my birthday, Wednesday October 1st.

Princess Joy is a beautiful 14-year old. I started sponsoring her in 2011, and she is now sponsored by my friend Dani Moore. I can honestly say that out of all my sponsored kids over the last few years, Princess's letters were my favorite. They were always two pages long, honest, detailed and written in her developing English.

I met Princess and her mother in Manila in 2013, but we did not really get the chance to talk much or get to know each other because we were always so busy on the day and I met three kids at once. Princess constantly mentioned her family's poor financial state in her letters, so I really wanted to see her neighborhood and community for myself.

Princess Joy is one of seven kids. She is the fourth-born, smack bang in the middle. I was incredibly blessed to meet all seven siblings on this day. The oldest is JoJo. He is 25 and pumps gas at the local Petron gas station. He has a wife and a three-year-old boy, and his wife is studying Education at the local university. Next is Paul, who works for a local construction company. Third is Jhon, who works with JoJo at the gas station. Princess Joy is fourth in line and she is in eighth grade at the local high school. She wants to be a teacher. The younger three are Joselle (12), Lori (7) and Michael (5).

They live in the community of Maydolong, which is a good 40 minute tricycle ride from where I was staying in Borongan. I was picked up by Jimuel, the Project Director of PH862. The Project has been running for seven years and currently has 180 children, with a further quota of 60 additional 3-5 year olds in the near future. The communities of Borongan and Maydolong are right on the ocean, and were both greatly affected by Typhoon Haiyan in November 2013.

Today was not a Project activity day, so once we arrived at the Project I was serenaded by the Project staff (and Princess Joy) singing 'Happy Birthday' to me. I initially didn't recognize Princess, as she had grown so much in 18 months. We shared a big hug and I could tell it was going to be a special day for both of us.

We took a tour of the Project and I had a look at Princess's student folder. Comprehensive records of each child are kept, including letters and gifts received, medical, educational, home visits, the child's future goals and dreams. I showed her some pictures from her sponsor Dani, as well as some photos of the kids at Ruel.

The family's home situation is complex, and I will try my best to explain it here. They own one home about two minutes away from the Project. They lived there for about 20 years, and currently the oldest son JoJo lives there with his wife and three year old boy. The rest of them live out on a 'farm,' which is about a five-minute motorbike ride away. It is where

Princess's parents both work. They grow, buy and sell copra, which is found in coconuts.

I quickly sensed God's hand of provision and blessing on this family, despite their simple circumstances. All the family members who work are employed by a relative; he was described as the second cousin of Princess's father. This same person owns the Petron gas station where the older boys work, as well as the farm where the parents work and the family also lives. So, thanks to this one relative the family have jobs as well as a place to live.

The house on the farm is basically a one-room open shelter with few facilities or amenities, but they seem content there. From what I could see there was no electricity, and they had to fetch their water for washing and cooking. The house on the farm was completely destroyed during Typhoon Haiyan, but the owner had it rebuilt as soon as he could. While the house was rebuilt, they stayed in a building next to the Petron gas station.

We were able to visit the house as well as the farm, and had some enjoyable conversations. They were all easy to talk to, and there were lots of kids to interact with and make funny faces at. Princess's father climbed a coconut tree and got a couple down just for me. The glass of juice I drank was humbling because I knew those coconuts are their livelihood, so it was a sacrifice for them.

While we were at the house on the farm, I gave Princess a very special gift. After giving my toy dog Sam to my sponsored child Ana Cristina in 2012, the last remaining soft toy from my childhood was Yellow Ted, who I had since I was born and he was very precious to me. I made the decision a couple of weeks before the visit to give him to Princess Joy, as a symbol of how much I love her and also how much God loves her. The night before visiting Princess Joy I actually had second thoughts, but only for a moment. Yellow Ted had been such an integral part of my childhood and my life to that point. Could I really give him away? In the end the answer was 'yes', and I know that along with her three younger siblings they will take good care of my teddy bear.

For our last activity in Maydolong, we popped into the Petron gas station where Jhon, the third oldest son, was working. We had a short, friendly conversation and then along came Paul, on a break from his construction job. I never imagined that with such a big family I would be able to meet all the family members. It was very special, and I know God provided it for us.

Then it was time to head into Borongan for lunch. Along for the ride were Jimuel, Princess, her mother, her Project worker and her little brother Michael, who was overwhelmed out of his brain. He is five, but wouldn't even feed himself at lunch. His mum had to, and for the first ten minutes he wouldn't even open his mouth. Thankfully, by the end of the day he had warmed up. In hindsight I'm not sure why the two younger sisters missed out, and if I had my time again I would have invited them along as well.

Princess told me her favorite food is spaghetti, and we ended up at 'Chicken Haus' where she was able to indulge in this wondrous meal. Next up was shopping. Her sponsor Dani had given a small monetary gift for the family to buy some groceries, and I chipped in to buy the kids one present each, since I had not brought any with me. The kids gift amount was equivalent to $25. Her mother bought a present each for the younger three and, being a teenage girl, Princess went to a few different shops before she was able to decide what she wanted.

To be honest I completely understood her indecisiveness over her sudden abundance of choice. The family had only ever window-shopped at this mall, and now she had a three-figure peso amount to spend on whatever she wanted. She looked at shoes, jewelry and clothes, but in the end she decided on that staple item of all teenage girls these days, a cellphone. She was very excited, and seeing the joy on her face alone was worth the expense (which was less than $20).

Jimuel asked my permission before they bought it, because he said a cellphone is not normally a 'necessity' item they would buy with sponsors birthday or Christmas gift money. Because I was there in person and it was my money, I was fine with it. I am trusting that it will not become a disruption or a distraction for Princess Joy in her studies or relating to her family. Maybe I'm being naïve?

After the gifts and groceries at the mall I gave Princess a choice between going to a swimming pool or the beach, and she chose the beach. It's interesting how attitudes towards beaches differ in the Philippines compared to Australia. In Australia beaches are more popular for day trips and because you can lie on the sand and tan your skin darker. In the Philippines people want to be whiter, so they stay out of the sun as much as possible. Also, the most popular beaches have cottages and hotels on them so people can stay for extended vacations.

The Borongan beach was completely deserted, even though it was a superb day with clear blue skies and the sun beating down. Princess and I, accompanied by Jimuel, headed out to the water. We stood in the shallows, letting the water wash over our feet. We kicked up mud and buried our feet in the sand. We talked about school, friends, television shows and creatures that live in the ocean. It was such a simple time, but Princess said it was her favorite part of the day.

We finished off with ice creams back at the mall and then said our goodbyes. My final message to Princess was simple: *"I love you, your sponsor Dani loves you, and most importantly God loves you. He is the one who brought us together. Please remember, no matter how hard your life gets, that God loves you and has a plan for your life."*

And thus ended another incredible birthday, the fourth one in the last six years I have spent visiting my Compassion kids. Devoting my life to giving to others is incredibly fulfilling, and for me there is no price tag you can put on it. At the end of my life I may not have much to my name materially, but through the sacrifices I have made I know I have helped create memories and experiences for many people and planted the seed of God's love in many hearts.

Someone Loves Wendy

I wanted to share with you a story that has captivated me ever since I first read it. It was written by a young woman named Emily, who authors a blog called "An Ounce of Compassion" and it was reproduced on the Compassion International blog on October 30, 2012.

It is written as a fictional story, but truthfully it could be the story of thousands of children around the world. Poverty breeds feelings of anger, failure, shame and hopelessness, right from when a person is very young. This is the story of 8-year-old Wendy as she goes from hopeless failure to a future filled with hope as a Compassion sponsored child.

I know I will never be wanted; something deep down inside, tells me so. Each time the cold eyes of my papa chisel at my heart, I know I am nothing but shame to him. I am desperate, oh so desperate for his approval, the love that he forever withholds from me. It shatters my heart into a million tiny pieces that no one can put back into place. He is ashamed of my weakness. I try to be strong. I struggle to pull the tears back, but they so easily rebel. I cannot do better and I know *I am a failure*.

The coldness of solitude creeps into my bones as the echoes of laughter reach my ears. There is no room for me to partake in the laughter of my fellow school mates. I am too ashamed to make friends. I know they must despise me: a motherless creature, who fails before the eyes of both my teacher and Papa. As Teacher gathers her students back to the classroom, I slowly follow behind.

Nearing the doorway, my heartbeat nearly comes to a halt. I can barely take in a breath. My exam is today. Will I even pass into the next grade? Surely my Papa will be disappointed with me if I fail him again. He cannot waste his meager income on such a slow animal.

Each minute of the exam seems to stretch longer, as I scribble down answers. I strive to pull the facts from my brain. I struggle to comprehend. As my dull pencil gets shorter and shorter, the pink rubber eraser becomes worn with frequent use. Fear grips my heart and twists it relentlessly. My breaths are quick and short. My head is dizzy. My hardened brown feet kick the legs of the desk monotonously. A pestering fly teases me cruelly. The hot air chokes my attention. And yet all I can think about is Papa.

Papa, working hard on the farm to feed me and keep me in school; day after day, fighting the unyielding clay. If only he knew how I loved him so dearly, how very hard I try to please him. If only I had worked a little harder after school, it wouldn't have been my fault. I wouldn't have killed my dear sweet Mama, if only I had done more. She was too weak to work, but I hadn't known. How wicked I was to have stayed in school while Mama, suffering with cancer, labored at the farm. If only I had known how much pain she was experiencing, I would have worked harder. I would have exerted all of my eight-year-old strength, so that she could rest. I helped the best I knew how, but it wasn't enough. How can I expect Papa to forgive me, when I cannot forgive myself?

All at once, my thoughts fly back to the exam. The dryness in my throat makes it hard to swallow. With a minute left, I scratch out my name at the top of the paper and hand it in.

The walk home today is more painful than the hunger growing in my stomach. Fear whirls in my mind and each dusty step fills my heart with more dread. Approaching the stench of our small farm, I hear a pleading voice from behind the tarp. Whipping in the wind, it seals out very little sound. I know that my Abuela is speaking with Papa in the house. Her smooth words advocate for me.

"This will be good for Wendy, my son. Surely you can see that? Do not let your hardened heart stand in the way of her best interest."
"Her best interest? Have I not labored to keep her off the streets? She is a lazy child, who does not deserve to go to school. I cannot allow her to

attend a church program," his firm voice bellows above the loud flapping of the tarp.

"*I will not back down Juan,*" comes the quiet reply of my grandmother. Her weak voice trembles with earnest, and I yearn to be held in her arms. "*Wendy must be registered tomorrow for the Child Development Center. I believe that God has sent this opportunity to us.*"

Papa does not respond. His silence scares me. I creep closer, but terror prevents me from entering the small room where they converse. Finally his strong voice speaks.

"*If it gets her out of my sight,*" he retorts, "*you can take her tomorrow, but God has sent us nothing. He has only taken from me and my family.*"

Suddenly, the tarp flies back sharply, and Papa storms past. After observing me angrily, he disappears behind the rusty shed.

Taking Abuela's wrinkled hand, I step into a long line of waiting people. The children stare blankly at the splintered floor of our tiny church. Pastor Jose greets the crowd kindly. I tug Abuela's sleeve gently, fearing that she will become irritated with me. She turns her head and I can read the sympathy in her eyes.

"*Why are we here, with all of these people?*" I ask imploringly. She nods with patience and I wait for her response.

"*I am going to register you with the Compassion project here at Pastor Jose's church,*" her words come slow. "*This will help you greatly, my child.*" I want to believe her, but I am also puzzled. I know of a young girl in my school who attends the project once a week. She talks about her sponsor and shares about the activities and games she plays at the Center. She says because of her sponsor, her family is now able to buy groceries and provide her a uniform. And still, I do not know what to expect.

We talk with several people and answer many questions. Then I am whisked away with a number of other children and each of our pictures are taken. I have never seen a camera before, although I have always wondered what they look like. Something that is able to capture the image of a person, must be truly magnificent. I stare at it wonderingly, as lights flash three times. It is almost a sort of magic I assume.

Abuela takes me home. I am very tired. Next week I will come to the project and meet my teacher. I want to be happy, but the truth haunts me. I know she will soon discover that I am a failure. I wonder if I must take many exams at the Project?

I have attended the project for many weeks. A new light is burning in my heart. At the project, we learn fascinating Bible stories and I am making new friends. I still don't have a sponsor, but the teacher has prayed that one will come soon! I am very happy.

I have passed the third year of primary school. I had hoped that this would make Papa glad, however most days he is silent. He will not speak to me, but I talk to him. I tell him all about the joy I have found at the project.

"Papa, today my teacher, Marie, taught us how God sent His Son Jesus all the way to this earth, just so He could die to save us from our sins. Do you think He did that for me too?" I beam with excitement. But Papa does not reply. My heart sinks with a heavy burden. I return to scrubbing his shirts. The soap stings my cut hands, so I quickly dip them into the cloudy water. Suddenly he speaks, but his words cut me like a knife. *"So is my daughter too stupid of a girl to deserve a sponsor? I knew no one would want you. It has been four months now, and no one has chosen you."* He turns to leave the room. I lower my head to hide the tears that stain my face and drip into the bucket of laundry.

I didn't think of it much before, but now, each day without a sponsor seems to pierce me deeper and deeper. One by one the other children in the Center find a sponsor, but I am left alone. I am too much of a failure for anyone to want me.

The rainy season soaks the world around me. Wet mud puddles stain my clothes, as I follow my grandmother to the church service. My mind
180

begs to silently slip into the back pew, but Abuela steadily presses toward the front. I gaze upward at the wooden cross which hangs majestically from one of the supporting beams. My step becomes lighter, and I sit on the front pew, beside my beloved Abuela. Her faithful eyes rest on Pastor Jose, who is opening his Bible and preparing to speak. I listen intently.

"Jesus loves you all so much. In fact, there is nothing you can do that is bad enough to remove His love. He is forever knocking at the door of your heart. He truly desires a relationship with you," Pastor Jose paused and gave his flock of sheep a genuine smile of love. He wanted so much to lead them on the right path. If only they would listen to his cries of sincerity. *"He wants to come into your hurting heart and fill it with His love. Please let Him in. Please don't keep Him waiting outside any longer."*

My heart slowly fills with hope as I hear the wonderful words of Pastor Jose. I never knew that Jesus would want someone like me. How could one so perfect, love a child as horrible as I? The question is rolling over and over in my head. But as I ponder this almost impossible statement, a feeling of love is beginning to surround me. I am beginning to realize that Jesus really does love me, even if no one else does.
I shyly rise from my seat and creep up to the Pastor after the service.
"Will you help me let Him in?" I stammer.
His smile pierces my hopeless heart. *"I would be more than happy to help you."*
Pastor Jose kneels beside me and leads me in a prayer filled with compassion. God's love pours in and washes away the sorrow. I am full of peace and joy. Maybe one day my papa will feel this peace as well.

The days pass by and I eagerly count each one. I am longing for the day when my sponsor will find me. At the project, Marie pulls me aside when it is time for the children to return to their homes.
"I have a gift for you," her voice dances with happiness. I take the small box she places in front of me. Inside is a beautiful black Bible, all my own. I have never held a Bible before, so I touch its smooth cover reverently. The soft paper feels so soothing between my rough fingertips. This Bible is a precious jewel to me; *my only possession.* Its

treasured words will lead me closer to *Him*, the one friend I have. The One who gave salvation to a failure.

"*And now*," she continues. "*I have some very special news for you, my little Wendy.*" Marie pauses and places her warm hand on my stooped shoulders. "*Someone has decided to sponsor you!*"

I take in a quick breath of thick air, my brown eyes fixed on the tiny letters of my Spanish Bible. At first, I do not look up into Marie's smiling face. But as her words sink in, gratefulness overflows the tiny cup of my heart. My brimming eyes turn upward.

They want me? I whisper with a cracked voice unlike my own. Marie nods.

They love me. I breathe.

There are thousands of children like Wendy around the world, caught in the traps of poverty, waiting for someone to help them. You can be the one who lifts them out and gives them hope, by sponsoring them through Compassion.

Jenny and Jessica: Two Stories of Rescue, Hope and Compassion

Dr Wess Stafford recently retired after serving for 20 years as Compassion's president. He spent his early years as a missionary kid in an African village and suffered horrendous abuse of many kinds at a mission boarding school. Remarkably, he is able to look back on that time in his life and see it as God preparing him for a life of serving the world's children with Compassion. He can relate to and identify with children in poverty who are abused, broken and vulnerable because he was one himself.

Dr Stafford has kindly given me permission to reproduce two of the stories featured in his book 'Just a Minute,' which is a collection of true stories highlighting the significant opportunities and responsibility we have in impacting the lives of the children around us.

These stories feature two girls at opposite ends of the sponsorship journey. Jenny is a graduate who returns to her Project and is able to offer a powerful example of the impact Compassion has to the children who are just like she used to be. Jessica is a little girl just starting out and she experiences the rescue and healing of God through Compassion and the local church after she is raped in her neighbourhood.

Jenny in Bolivia – Hope Goes Full Circle
A few years ago I was visiting Compassion's work in Bolivia. One of our sponsored children named Jenny had not only graduated from our child development program but had been selected for our Leadership Development Program — a very select group sent on to university.

Jenny came from a poor family who lived in the high altitude of the Andes Mountains. It had always been Jenny's dream to be a nurse — but that would be a real stretch. After all, her father fixed bicycles for a living. She had studied hard as a child, however, and managed to get accepted into La Paz University's School of Nursing.

Moving away from her little adobe home high in the mountains to live in the big city was scary. The academics were daunting. When she wrote to her sponsors pleading for their prayer support, their replies always carried the same message: *"We are so very proud of you, Jenny. You can do this. Look how far you've come. Sweetheart, don't give up...do your best."*

Jenny listened, was encouraged, and worked diligently. Not only was she about to graduate as a full-fledged nurse, but she would also graduate first in her class! She had competed with the children of Bolivia's elite and powerful families and had come out on top. Jenny's sponsors had traveled all the way from Oregon to honor and celebrate her achievement.

As Jenny took us on a tour of the nursing school, her sponsors were so proud of her. She was obviously loved and respected by teachers and everyone we met. Then we made the arduous trip to the Compassion child development center where Jenny had been nurtured. It was a jostling two-mile Jeep ride — a journey she had made on foot every day of her childhood. When we arrived at the little mud church, nobody was expecting our visit. As Jenny and three very strange-looking people walked in together, the peasant pastor looked up, surprised.

Then, recognizing his former student in her pristine white nurse's uniform, he remembered her love for the guitar and her lovely voice. *"Welcome back, Jenny!"* he cried. *"Come, please sing a song for the children."*

The children, about a hundred of them, were sitting on narrow, rough-hewn benches, pressed tightly together. Like chickens on a roost, I thought. They were so cute. Everything was brown — the floor, the walls, the children, even their clothes — except for Jenny's uniform.

The children cheered in excitement. About halfway through her song, I noticed Jenny as she looked, her eyes fixed, at just one place. Then I saw a tear trickle down her beautiful face. In a minute, I could see the object of her gaze: a little girl at the end of the third row. The girl was so small that her feet were swinging above the dirt floor.

Suddenly Jenny's voice cracked. Tears filled her eyes and she stopped singing. *"Sweetheart,"* I heard her say softly to that little girl, *"that's where I used to sit when I was little like you. You are sitting in my place. Do you see what has happened to me? That can happen to you — don't ever, ever give up! Just always do your best …."*

At that moment, Jenny looked up and across to the back of the church. I watched as her eyes met the eyes of her sponsors. The same message, still alive! That's all I saw, because just then…well, everything went blurry for me.

I am so deeply grateful to all of you who sponsor children with Compassion. You are paying attention to the "construction zones" God places in your path. You are blessing not only your sponsored children, but also those whose lives are touched by them, including the next generation. You are building role models! It is my prayer that the ripples from all your moments of building and blessing in children's lives will roll gently on, all the way to the shores of heaven.

Little Jessica – Broken But Healed and Restored With Compassion
You never quite know when a young life is hanging by a thread, physically or otherwise, and your intervention will make a major difference. I've seen it happen time and again.

One of my most precious Compassion moments was on the far side of the world, in Manado, Indonesia. The little church I entered that day was constructed of weather-beaten, hand-hewn wood from the surrounding jungle. The 100 or so children had gathered in the sanctuary and were all sitting cross- legged on the wood floor, their eyes eager to see these strange visitors who had arrived. Their teachers stood along the walls; mothers and a few fathers gathered shyly at the back of the room.

The children sang and danced and recited Scripture and poetry for us. So poor, yet so precious in every way. Then I was asked if I wanted to say a few words to them. I thought fast. What could I say to let them know how precious they were, how loved by Compassion, by their little church…as well as their sponsors on the other side of the world?

I started in a lighthearted vein:
"In all the world I have never seen a place with such beautiful children!" I exclaimed. *"Your parents must be so very proud of you! You produce such lovely singing. And all those Bible verses! You must be very, very smart."* The children giggled. The teachers were smiling, eyes twinkling with gratitude. The poverty-stricken parents looked at their little ones with newfound respect and pride.
"Does anybody know what you want to be when you grow up?" I asked. A few brave hands went up.
"A soldier," one boy said.
"A policeman," said another.
"A teacher," added a third. The adults beamed.
"A pastor," said a fourth.
I pointed out a little boy and said *"I think I see a future doctor."* He grinned. *"And look!"* I continued. *"Somewhere in this room might be a future president of Indonesia! Do you know which one? No? Well you'd better treat every child here like you would the President of your country, because you never know!"* The room buzzed with excitement.

In the very front row, sitting at my feet, was a beautiful but frail little girl, maybe six years old. Her eyes were looking up at me wide in wonder. She was too shy to have shouted out any dreams. My heart paused for a moment. I had an idea.
"Do you know how precious you all are to God? He knows you and loves more than anything else in the whole world. Like this little girl…" I knelt down and gently lifted her up in my arms. *"Do any of you know her name?"*

"*Jessica*," they all called out. I looked at her face and she shyly nodded; they had it right.

"*Jesus knows Jessica's name*," I said. "*But do any of you know how many hairs she has on her head*?" Silence.

"*Jesus does! He loves little Jessica so much that He keeps track of everything about her, even the number of hairs on her head. Did you ever look closely at the tips of your fingers? See those tiny lines, that little design? Jesus made every one of you unique, special.*" I took Jessica's little fingers in my hands. "*God loved Jessica so much he drew her very own picture on her fingers like nobody else's in the whole world.*" Jessica looked intently at her fingers, until a shy smile formed. She snuggled deeper into my arms.

"*God loved her before she was even born. He knit her in her mama's womb. And look-He made her beautiful, gave her her very own laugh, her beautiful eyes. He knows exactly what she will be when she grows up. She has no idea how special she is to God, and how loved. Jesus would have died on the cross for her even if she was the only child on earth!*"

The room grew suddenly quiet. As I glanced around at the teachers, I saw eyes brimming. A tear trickled down the craggy face of the peasant pastor beside me. Something seemed to be happening here…

I laid my hand on little Jessica's head and prayed. I thanked God for every child in that church, but especially for Jessica's life and for loving her so much. Then I moved to place her back on the floor where I'd found her. But her arms held tightly around my neck. Slowly, reluctantly, she released me. In her eyes I saw tears like those of the teachers. What was going on here? What had turned the party atmosphere into a somber moment?

I returned to my chair to sit down. A few minutes later the pastor leaned over to whisper, "*You couldn't possibly have known, but if ever a little girl needed to be lovingly held and affirmed, it was Jessica right now.*"

Why was that? Before leaving the place, the staff told me with broken hearts that just a month or so earlier, little Jessica had been savagely raped by a man in her neighborhood. She had been so violated that she needed surgery, stitches and hospitalization. The pastor and the church had courageously pressured the legal authorities on her behalf. But the man had gotten off with no penalty, no jail, nothing – by paying a bribe of just $300.

The little church was devastated. Once again in poverty, justice had failed, and the poor had paid the price. An innocent little girl had suffered the brutality of a world that has lost its heart. *"We are amazed that she would even let you, a man, pick her up and hold her in your arms,"* the teachers said.

Years have passed since that incident, and I am told that our brief moment together was the beginning of her healing. She is beginning to blossom again in mind, soul and spirit.

Sowing Seeds of Generosity and Gratitude –Sharing Compassion

My life as a Compassion sponsor has coincided nicely with my career as a teacher. It is indeed a privileged position to hold. I have taught primary/elementary classes in Australia at several different schools over the last few years, and it has been an absolute joy to be able to share the lives of my Compassion kids with my students.

I have shared with my students the names of all my sponsored kids, told them stories about their lives, shown them photos and we have written them letters. My goal was to show them how children in other parts of the world live, that we need to be thankful to God for what we have and help other people any way we can.

I have been thrilled to hear when my students have told me their family sponsored a child because I know that a seed of generosity has been planted in many little hearts and they in turn will impact others. Little by little, lives will be transformed and the world may become a slightly better place. Who knows? Can't hurt to try.

In 2011 I taught a combined Grade 1/2 class at a wonderful Lutheran school. This class in particular was very enthusiastic about my family of Compassion children. Many people in the school community knew about my passion for sponsorship, yet I didn't push or promote Compassion in the school at all because I knew the Lutherans have their own organization called Australian Lutheran World Service. I understand that this school has now taken on and embraced Compassion in a much larger and more meaningful way. My heart rejoiced.

I love hearing people say *"because of your story, I decided to sponsor a child."* It's happened a few times. Those words motivate me in my advocacy because it means other people are joining me in the amazing life-transforming journey that is Compassion sponsorship. In 2012 I shared at my new school about my involvement with Compassion. A wonderful colleague named Steve went home and told his family around the dinner table and right then, unprompted, his 15-year-old daughter made the decision to use some of the earnings from her part-time job to sponsor a child.

I have never shied away from telling my Compassion kids about the rest of my Compassion family. Whenever I sponsored more kids I would make up a photo collage, send it to the existing kids, introduce the new ones and ask them to pray for each other. Some sponsors of multiple kids have reservations about telling them about each other but I have never had any negative reactions from any of the kids. I emphasize that they are part of a great big family that God has brought together and He loves them all very much.

An amazing moment occurred when one of my sponsored kids wrote to me and said "*I want to sponsor children like you do.*" That's what it's all about.

2013 was a big year in terms of my advocacy. I was twice able to share Compassion with a group of 9th and 10th grade students at my school. They had been sponsoring a teenage boy as a class and apparently had struggled to find the motivation to come up with the very miniscule monthly amount needed to support him. I was able to go in first thing on a Tuesday morning and give them a bit of a wake-up call I suppose, to make it real for them. I hope that sharing some of my experiences and the reality of the lives of those kids can maybe inspire these students to help others and demonstrate a spirit of generosity in their own lives.

After I returned from the Philippines in April 2013 I prayed for opportunities to share my experiences. Very soon after, I got a call from Compassion regarding Compassion Sunday which is a day where advocates all over Australia go into their churches and raise awareness for Compassion child sponsorship. The Lutheran church in Portland, which is the little town where I had lived previously, was looking for someone to do a Compassion Sunday presentation but all the Victorian staff were already busy that day. Would I be willing to go? I didn't need too long to think about that.

So I headed down to Portland and spoke at the two morning services at the Lutheran church. It was a small gathering and many of them already sponsored children, but five children were sponsored that day. Five more little lives starting the journey away from poverty and towards hope. Five more sponsors obeying the call of God.

Before my trip to South America in September 2013 I told my Grade 1 class *"If you have any toys at home that you don't use and you would like to give them to my Compassion kids, bring them to school."* The result was a big fat bulging suitcase filled with toys, dolls and books, and a $170 excess baggage fee. Totally worth it! Generosity in action from little hearts filled with love.

In 2014 when I was in the Philippines, I was contacted by some friends in Australia, Bek and Gary McClellan, about contributing to their church's Compassion Sunday in August. This was to be in the form of a long-distance interview about my Compassion journey and work with Ruel, to be viewed during the 'kid's talk' time. They sent me a video of their nine-year-old daughter "Roving Reporter Ruby Rose" asking the questions, and I sent back a video of my responses.

I was told it got some laughs and challenged many people as well. Ten more kids were sponsored by the end of the day and quite a few others took information home with them to seriously consider sponsorship. I was excited and humbled even to play a little part in that.

In the News—For Your Glory God

In 2012 I lived in a little town in south-west Victoria which had quite a challenging spiritual climate. When I was in Brazil in September, my friend Karen contacted the local newspaper and suggested my Compassion trip as a story idea. I was contacted by the newspaper and sent back a spiel outlining who Compassion is, as well as a bit about my Compassion journey. I did not hide away from my true motivation: that I do it because of God's love for me and I want to use what I have been given to help others.

Three days after I arrived back in Australia there was a nice half-page spread in the Wednesday edition and they had included *everything* I wrote, including the God references, which to me was a triumph. I don't know what came from people seeing the article but I hope at the very least it got people thinking *"Oh, maybe Christians aren't all _____"* (insert preconceived negative ideas here) and they are also now aware of Compassion.

For a period of time, God put Compassion and child sponsorship on my heart so fully that I financially sponsored 50 kids from 26 countries (don't bother doing the math). I also visited 31 of those kids in 12 countries. I guess this kind of lifestyle is pretty rare, so it was bound to catch people's attention sooner or later.

In 2011 I was talking about Compassion to a relative named Chad Loftis. Chad is a journalist, documentary maker and media guy, and he expressed interest in doing a mini-documentary about my sponsorship journey. It ended up happening in May 2012 and involved Chad and another friend Simon coming down to the sleepy little town where I lived, filming some of my normal day and doing a sit-down interview.

He also interviewed my parents who, at that time, were having trouble coming to terms with my lifestyle choice of God-inspired sacrificial generosity (they have come around and have since sponsored two of my kids). The editing and producing process took a bit longer, with Chad raising four kids with his wife, and his family moving to Thailand with a missionary organization.

Chad had planned to release it mid-2013 but around that time Compassion Australia contacted me about featuring in an article in the September edition of the Compassion magazine. They got in contact with Chad and it was decided to release both the documentary and the article at the same time in September 2013. To make things more interesting, at this exact time I was in South America on another Compassion trip and writing about it on Facebook and my blog.

It was quite surreal. Because of the nature of social media, literally thousands of people were seeing my story. I was told they watched it in a staff meeting at Compassion Australia HQ, which is quite humbling. The attention was enjoyable for the little while it lasted and the encouragement I received from many people was great, but I can honestly say that's never been a motivating factor in my involvement with Compassion.

I've had my heart and motives questioned by people close to me, but all that matters is what God thinks. I am confident I can appear before God and my motives and heart will be revealed to be clean; that I've done it all for the right reasons and I have eternal treasure stored for me in heaven.

I want to see kids sponsored.
I want to see lives transformed.
I want God to be glorified through it all.
I want people, when they see my life of sacrificial generosity, to see God in me.

Innermost Thoughts From the 'Bubble of Blessing'

In 2012, at the height of the 'Compassion madness' I was living in a small country town and sponsoring 50 children from all 26 Compassion countries. It was a challenging year in some ways but I was living in what I called a 'bubble of blessing', surrounded by an inexplicable sense of peace and contentment. I could literally feel God honouring the sacrifices I was making in denying myself and doing my best to live for Him. One night I scribbled down some thoughts:

I am in an incredible place right now. Peace and contentment beyond what I've ever had, or ever will have on this earth. I know I'm where I'm supposed to be, doing what I'm supposed to do.

I'm well aware that this is because I'm being sustained by the prayers of countless of the world's poor in 26 countries – at least 50 children, possibly their parents and siblings, possibly other children and staff at the Compassion Centers which offer an oasis of hope to these kids, and it's purely because of the grace and mercy of God.

Never before have I been so sure of anything – be it my gifts and talents or the reason for my existence. I am using what I've been given by God to make my 'drop in the ocean' and fight against child poverty and the hurt, despair and hopelessness that comes with it. I have made it my business to make poverty personal – its victims have names, faces and a future in God. It's hurting my heart and spirit, but it's okay because I know it affects God in the same way, on a much larger scale. He truly is breaking my heart for what breaks His.

Living for myself and spending what I've been given on myself only, in order to make my life more comfortable is now inconceivable to me. It's not even an idea I would contemplate. I have one foot in now and one foot in eternity. Because right now I have finances and health and resources, I want to use it to bring glory to God by making an eternal difference in people's lives. I'm not going to wait until I have 'more' or 'enough' because if I keep putting it off, that day may never come. I cannot take for granted that I will live a long life. I look at the news and every day there are stories of lives cut tragically short. Without being morbid, that could be me, so I'm doing what I can NOW to make a difference.

If God's plan is for me to live until 80 (though I don't really want to), I know He will provide my needs and more because He has promised to IF I am faithful with what he gives me, which I believe I am being. I have discovered the satisfaction and contentment Paul talked about in the Good Word – I am happy with a roof over my head, food on the table and clothes on my back, which is why I can spend over half my income on others.

I do not desire material possessions. They hold no appeal to me. Last Christmas I was loaded up with a stack of gift cards and wandered around aimlessly because there was nothing I really needed or desperately wanted.

Playing music and teaching – both things I feel I've been created to do, yet polar opposites. Music comes so naturally to me – purely God-given, everything – pitch, beat, rhythm. I am 'musical' to my bones and the very fabric of my being. Not a bass or drum lesson in my life, yet when I hear something, I play it. How can something be so instinctive, so intuitive? If I were to earn my living playing music it would be the best life ever – so good!

Teaching is a different story. While I believe I was created to teach, every day is a struggle. There are parts I love – mainly the daily interaction with the kids, those wonderful creations of God (though I sometimes don't feel that way about them), their innocence, joy, enthusiasm, affection and curiosity make every day a new adventure (as clichéd as that sounds). However, the nuts and bolts – planning, curriculum, assessment, reporting - is something I've never quite got my head around, which worries me because that's the 'important' stuff. That struggle has made me earn my money, as I have to work hard every day and it has made me grow, both as a person and professionally.

I love being able to sow the Word of God in little hearts. That is the most important thing for me and that is all I can do. We can't force them to believe but we can show them what a genuine, authentic Christian life looks like, then allow them to make up their own minds.

I am humbled, honoured and privileged that God has led me down this path and has allowed me, through Compassion sponsorship and teaching, to have a lasting, permanent and indelible impact on, so far, hundreds of children in such a short time. It's a huge responsibility and it kind of makes my head spin. I know much will be demanded of me when I have to give account of my life to God.

I would sum up my purpose to this point as three-fold – to inspire, encourage and challenge others. I want to be an example of how if you step out in faith and do something for God that others might see as crazy, He will honour you and always provide for your needs.

A Tribute to True Heroes

The word 'hero' gets thrown around a lot and is very subjective. It means different things to different people. To me, a hero is someone I look up to and want to be like. Someone who inspires and challenges me. Heroes sacrifice for the good of others. There is always a cost involved in heroism – putting the needs of others before your own.

In my travels with Compassion I have met true heroes–the Pastors and Compassion Project workers who, with God's help, battle against the formidable enemy of poverty and all that comes with it. Hopelessness. Despair. Violence. Hunger. Illness and Disease. Family disintegration. This is their daily battle.

I am always so inspired by the Compassion staff, both at the Projects and in the country office. They literally give their lives for the families and children they serve. The majority of Compassion Project workers are volunteers from the local church and yet they serve so joyfully, with a servant heart. Many of them are professionals who could easily be getting more money/recognition/status etc. elsewhere but choose to put all that aside and spend their lives sharing God's love with the poorest of the poor by serving with Compassion.

One testimony to the impact Compassion and the local church has on people's lives is that without fail, at every Project I've been to there are formerly sponsored children who return to volunteer at the Project in some form-whether they're teaching a class, teaching a musical instrument, cooking the food or giving medical care.

They don't just come back because they have nothing better to do, but they want to be a living example to the kids. To give the kids the hope of God and be able to say *"Look what God has done in my life. I used to be a sponsored child like you, but He has rescued me and given me a hope and a purpose, and He can do the same for you."*

It has been a privilege for me to be able to pray with and for these amazing people and encourage them every opportunity I get. One particular conversation broke my heart. One lady was in tears while she shared with me the challenges her community faces. She added they sometimes wonder if anyone does remember them and pray for them. They often feel forgotten.

So, I want to draw attention to the sacrificial and heroic work of the Compassion Project workers. Not so they get worldly recognition or kudos. That's not what they want. But so that we who are Christians and/or sponsors can keep them in our prayers, regularly lift them up to God and maybe even encourage them in the letters we write to our sponsor children.

God is using them, as well as those of us who are sponsors, to transform the lives of children and families and release them from poverty in Jesus name.

Stories from the Compassion Projects and Beyond

It is fair to say I am not an investigative type of person. I don't ask a lot of questions.

Example:
Me: "I saw Fred Smith today." (*family friend from a few years ago*)
Mum: "Oh really? What's he up to these days?"
Me: "I don't know, I didn't really ask."

As a result, I've often left a day at a Compassion Project not knowing too much more than when I went in or I've neglected to write stuff down then forgotten it. However, I have managed to retain some Compassion Project stories and I'd like to share them here.

GU-400, Rain of Blessings
Each Compassion Project has a unique code and name in order to identify it. For example, 15-year-old Josefa in Guatemala attends GU-400, Rain of Blessings Project. She lives in a Mayan community out in the mountains and the Project was probably one of the more struggling, under-resourced ones I'd visited. When I visited the Guatemala Compassion Office I met the country director of Compassion Guatemala and he shared that for a few months the staff of that Project had been meeting regularly at a nearby Volcano to pray for the children, families and sponsors. Since they had started doing this, the children at the Project had received an increased number of letters, gifts and visits. Rain of Blessings indeed!

CO-335, So Few Caring For So Many
In 2013 I visited Laura at CO-335 in South Bogota, Colombia. It is a fairly dodgy area, as evidenced by the fact it took us five tries to get a taxi to take the family from the mall we visited back to their home. No-one wanted to go there! The area is notorious for gangs and robberies, and even Laura and her brother had been robbed of everything including their shoes on their way to school one day. With this in mind, when

I heard that the church attached to the Project has 70 members and they care for 350 kids I was blown away. As if I needed any more proof that Compassion is God's business.

BR-458, Modern-Day Loaves and Fishes Moment

Projeto Sementinhas (Little Seeds Project) is located just outside Fortaleza, Brazil and it is where I sponsor Jessica, Christian and Ana Cristina. I have visited this wonderful place twice, exactly one year apart in September 2012 and September 2013. On my first visit they were rebuilding the church and let's just say it was a work-in-progress. Three unfinished brick walls, no roof, building materials everywhere, basically a construction zone. It was also the only place the kids had to play. I was looking forward to seeing the progress but I had no idea how magnificent it would look.

I asked how they managed to do so much in a year, thinking Compassion or some other benefactor might have given a generous donation. I was not prepared for the answer: it was funded completely from the tithes and offerings of the church members. I nearly fell over. I guess to understand my shock you have to understand the challenges faced by the community, as told by the Pastor:

> *Geographically, we are located in the border of two cities: Fortaleza (the capital) and the outskirts of Caucaia. It is an area with absolute extreme poverty. In one side, we have Maranguapinho River with its signs of degradation. It almost dries up during the dry weather season, and it suffers with the untreated sewage that is thrown in it and the industrial illegal effluent. In addition, many families live by its margins at the risk of getting their houses flooded, but also contribute to the dump of garbage in it. In the other side, the swamp areas are compromised because it is used as a landfill, and the uneven occupation on its margins. These factors contribute to a social chaos whose main victim is the child. Since it is a risky area, there is not industrial or commercial investment which generates a high rate of unemployment. Because of the disqualified labor, women search for jobs as maids or cleaning ladies while men stay at home "looking after" the children and the house. Most families are unstructured, and there*

is a high number of single mothers living with stepfathers. As a consequence, children get vulnerable and insecure. The idleness leads them to gambling, drugs and other social illnesses.

This is a desperately poor and dangerous community. I know because I was there; I experienced it. The family of one of my sponsored children just recently moved back there, only because the work dried up and they couldn't afford to stay where they were. And yet God used the tithes and offerings of the church members of this community to reconstruct their church in one year. I couldn't help but think of this as a modern-day version of Jesus using five loaves of bread and two fish to feed thousands. Amazing.

Philippines: A Father's Testimony

When I was in the Philippines, a father shared his testimony in a church we visited. It was a truly profound moment for many of us who heard it. It is well-known that fathers are becoming an 'endangered species,' particularly in developing countries when it becomes apparent they can no longer provide for their families. This father plucked up all the courage he could muster, stood in a church filled with mothers, babies, kids and foreign guests and shared his testimony. He was a factory worker and used to beat and abuse his wife and kids (three boys and a little girl). He contracted tuberculosis of the bowel and became so sick he had to give his family to his brother, who was a Christian. During his illness the father gave his life to God. He admitted it was initially an insurance policy, since he thought he was going to die. However, over time God healed him completely and he stood in this church, vulnerable and open, and declared that he was a new creation and God had set him free. This will stay with me for a long time.

"What Are The Odds?" in Bangladesh

In 2012 I sponsored a child in Bangladesh called Monika. I received an email from a Compassion friend who went on a group tour to Bangladesh. She had some news for me: In a country of 150 million people, on their travels they happened to meet the man who translated the letters I wrote to Monika. What are the odds?

Compassion Australia "100,000 Sponsored Children" Celebration
In 2012, Compassion Australia passed the milestone of having 100,000 sponsored children and held a nice little event to celebrate it. Compassion is blessed to partner with many high profile musicians, artists and sportspeople and I knew they'd all be there. Me? I'm just a regular Joe, yet I somehow managed to score an invite in the mail.

It was on a Friday night in Newcastle, New South Wales (I lived in the state of Victoria) but I did not hesitate to take the day off work and catch a plane in order to attend. Above all else I was very keen to meet Dr. Wess Stafford, who is the former president of Compassion (retired 2013) and a very inspirational man. It says a lot about the man that he was the President of an organization that works in over 30 countries, yet he flew all the way from the US to be at our celebration. I'm sure people would have been happy with a video message.

I travelled up with a fellow Compassion sponsor from Victoria and on the way we talked about what the chances were of meeting Dr. Stafford, since he was the President and a very popular and in-demand person. When we arrived we noticed he only had two people around him.

I was so happy to be able to introduce myself and tell Dr. Stafford a bit about my sponsorship journey and how his love for children and for God had impacted me. I told him how many kids I sponsored at the time and was quite tickled when he turned to some people nearby, pointed me out and said *"This guy sponsors 49 kids!"* I was introduced to Mark Hanlon who is one of the Senior Vice Presidents, as well as Laurie McCowan, the man who founded Compassion Australia in 1977 along with his wife Olive.

Suddenly the event was about to start and I found myself sitting in the second row! It was a fantastic evening celebrating with like-minded Compassion sponsors, employees and advocates, marveling at what God had done and was continuing to do in and through us in the fight against poverty.

Giving Sam Away–An Act of Joyful Sacrifice

When I was six I was in hospital twice in the space of a year for tonsillitis and appendicitis. My family got me a toy dog as a present. My three-year-old brother had already called him Ben but I decided to name him Sam. Sam became very dear to me, along with my teddy bear Yellow Ted, and I kept them both well into adulthood.

In 2011 I sent my Compassion kids a photo of me holding my two beloved soft toys. In one of her rare letters, Ana Cristina from Brazil asked "*Will I play with them one day?*" When I visited her I was privileged to be able to give Cristina my toy dog Sam as a gift. It was a joyful act of sacrifice.

When I handed Sam over to her, just like the rest of the day she didn't say much, but I could see in her eyes she had an inkling how significant this gift was. I hope that in the many hard times she faces, Sam provides her with some measure of security and comfort and she is able to fix her mind on the one true sacrifice: Jesus given for us so that we are made right with God and can spend eternity with Him.

Katherine's New Sponsor – A God Connection
In November 2013 I was looking for new sponsors for all my kids, since I was going to be volunteering at an orphanage in the Philippines. I talked to a wonderful El Salvadorian friend, Milton Fuentes and his wife Cristina, about sponsoring Katherine from El Salvador. I felt that they could also be positive role models for Katherine's parents and encourage them in their marriage. Something I only realized after they agreed to the sponsorship blew me right away: Katherine's last name is *Fuentes Martinez*. Milton's last name is *Fuentes* and Cristina's maiden name was *Martinez*! God connection, pure and simple.

South Korea – From Receiving Help to Giving It
If there is one story that illustrates God's transforming power through Compassion, it is South Korea. Compassion began helping children in South Korea all the way back in 1952. 52 years later in 2004, they became a Compassion partner country and today over 123,000 children are sponsored *by* people in Korea. It's the ultimate circle of hope – from a

nation of sponsored kids, the ones receiving the help to being sponsors, the ones giving the help.

The Great Visit Debate

I have witnessed an interesting 'debate' of sorts among sponsors. It is along the lines of "*If I had the money, would it be better used on a trip to visit my sponsored child or on staying where I am and sponsoring more children?*"

To me, the answer is a no-brainer and a no-contest: visit!! Before I give some incredibly convincing reasons why, let me just clarify -I understand there are people who can't afford it, are unable or unwilling to fly and there are health/safety concerns etc. Ultimately it is completely between you and God.

However, for pure life-changing impact you can't go past a sponsor visit. You will literally never be the same again. You are stretched in every way possible. Your attitudes and expectations are put to the test. How do you react if things don't go the way you hoped? I've had more than my fair share of those and quite often been found wanting. Your motivations are revealed. Why are you doing this? To get something back in return or to demonstrate the selfless, sacrificial love of God?

Young Woman in Brazil
I met a young woman at Project BR-329 in Brazil in 2012. She is no longer in the program because her family is now self-sufficient and it is all because of a sponsor visit. Her sponsor came from the US and she was in the army. The sponsor started talking to her mother about her army experiences and the mother was motivated to join the Brazilian army. This decision was the catalyst to lift their family out of poverty. Sponsor visit = lives transformed.

Dreams Fulfilled!
It is safe to say that the biggest dream of the vast majority of sponsored children is to meet their sponsor in person. I've had it expressed to me so many times in the kid's letters. By visiting, God was using me to actually make their dream come true! Can you get your head around that?

Princess Joy
When I visited 12-year-old Princess Joy in the Philippines, I asked if she ever imagined I would come to visit. She shook her head, no. It was literally beyond her sphere of imagination or dreaming. That is how significant a sponsor visit is.

Josefa
After I visited her, 15-year-old Josefa from Guatemala wrote: "*I pray for you every day because now I know that dreams can come true asking God with all the heart.*" My decision to visit her actually strengthened her faith in God. This is a girl with four younger brothers and sisters who has to work making shoes for six hours a day to support her family because her father is an alcoholic.

Carolina
In January 2013 I visited 18-year-old Carolina in the Dominican Republic. It wasn't overly outstanding, exciting, action-packed or joyful. It was real life. There was awkwardness, silence, honesty and there were hard questions asked and answered.

It was evident right from the start that I should put this visit in the "*I know she enjoyed it but she didn't really show it*" category. I could not get a peep out of her and she stretched and exhausted my limited conversational skills.

Carolina is the third of a tribe of nine kids, aged 9 to 23. **It was sad to see her unable to answer questions about her dreams, what she likes to do or is good at. She seemed to lack direction and purpose.** She also mentioned at the start she was not a Christian, despite being in the Project since she was four and her family attends the church attached to the Compassion Project. This stuck with me and was the catalyst for our powerful farewell.

Before I left, I asked her "*What is the one thing stopping you from fully giving your life to God?*" She couldn't really answer. She was so close but there was just this barrier in the way. I shared with her my experience.

When I left school I was not a Christian and I had no idea what to do with my life–I lacked direction and purpose. As soon as I made the commitment at age 21, God started giving me opportunities and showed me what I should do with my life. That led to Compassion, teaching, music and basketball coaching.

I assured her that God loves her so much and His plan for her does not involve working for 40 years at a job she absolutely hates. That only happens when people choose to go their own way and make certain decisions in running their own life. I assured her that this decision to invite God in was completely up to her, and as soon as she made it He would start working in her life.

I then prayed for Carolina in the name of Jesus. I thanked Him for creating her and for His love for her. I thanked Him for giving her wisdom and asked him to remove that final barrier that is preventing her from committing her life fully to Him. I thanked Him for the future He had for her and for allowing me to play a part in her life. This was such a powerful time and it was a privilege. I could feel God stirring in her heart, inviting her to come to Him. Carolina was reduced to tears and I was pretty close.

I was overwhelmed by God's love for this young woman and for the fact that He used my visit to encourage her, to speak words of life to her in person, rather than on a page. I hoped this may even be the thing that 'pushed her over the edge' and helped her make the final step of faith to once and for all ask Jesus to be the Lord of her life.

It is the increasing knowledge and understanding of God's love that has compelled me to visit 31 kids in 12 countries. To me it has completed the connection. I wasn't satisfied with remaining some guy on the other side of the world. Indeed, even God wasn't content with remaining distant from the ones He loved – that's why He came to earth in the form of Jesus. Why shouldn't I do the same? The sacrifice Jesus made for us is far greater than any sacrifice I could make to go and visit my kids. It just made sense to me and I haven't regretted it one bit.

Postscript to this story: In November 2013 my friend Judy Myers took over sponsorship of Carolina, and she was able to visit her in in the Dominican Republic in April 2014. I was so happy to receive photos of her looking joyful and full of hope for the future. I learned she loves God and will be studying psychology at University.

The Good Word (Bible Verses)

One thing is clear from the Bible: God cares about the poor and the injustice in our world. Some people may say *"Well why doesn't He do something about it?"* That's where we come in. Because we live in a world affected by sin (rebellion against God), there is inequality and injustice on a massive scale. God has chosen to give some of us more than we need and He wants us to use those resources to care for the poor. Here are a few of my favorite verses that have inspired me to give generously and sacrificially for God's kingdom:

Oh, the joys of those who are kind to the poor! The Lord rescues them when they are in trouble. The Lord protects them and keeps them alive. He gives them prosperity in the land and rescues them from their enemies. The Lord nurses them when they are sick and restores them to health. (Psalm 41:1-3)

Give justice to the poor and the orphan; uphold the rights of the oppressed and the destitute. Rescue the poor and helpless; deliver them from the grasp of evil people. (Psalm 82:3-4)

All goes well for those who are generous, who lend freely and conduct their business fairly. Such people will not be overcome by evil circumstances... they will be long remembered. They confidently trust the Lord to care for them...they give generously to those in need...their good deeds will never be forgotten...they will have influence and honor. (Psalm 112:5-9)

It is possible to give freely and become more wealthy, but those who are stingy will lose everything (Proverbs 11:24)

The generous will prosper; those who refresh others will themselves be refreshed (Proverbs 11:25)

If you help the poor you are lending to the Lord, and He will repay you! (Proverbs 19:17)

Speak up for those who cannot speak for themselves; ensure justice for those being crushed. Yes, speak up for the poor and helpless, and see that they get justice. (Proverbs 31:8, 9)

Feed the hungry, and help those in trouble. Then your light will shine out from the darkness, and the darkness around you will be as bright as noon. The Lord will guide you continually, giving you water when you are dry and restoring your strength. You will be like a well-watered garden, like an ever-flowing spring (Isaiah 58:10)

He gave justice and help to the poor and needy, and everything went well for him. Isn't that what it means to know me?" says the Lord. (Jeremiah 22:16)

Now, O people, the Lord has told you what is good, and this is what he requires of you: to do what is right, to love mercy, and to walk humbly with your God. (Micah 6:8)

Give whatever you can according to what you have. If you are really eager to give, it isn't important how much you are able to give. God wants you to give what you have, not what you don't have. Of course, I don't mean that you should give so much that you suffer from having too little. I only mean that there should be some equality. Right now you have plenty and can help them. Then at some other time they can share with you when you need it. In this way, everyone's needs will be met. (2 Corinthians 8:11-14)

Remember this—a farmer who plants only a few seeds will get a small crop. But the one who plants generously will get a generous crop. You must each decide in your heart how much to give. And don't give reluctantly or in response to pressure. "For God loves a person who gives cheerfully." And God will generously provide all you need. Then you will always have everything you need and plenty left over to share with others. (2 Corinthians 9:6-8)

For God is the one who gives seed to the farmer and then bread to eat. In the same way He will give you many opportunities to do good and he will produce a great harvest of generosity in you. You will be enriched so that you can give even more generously. And when we take your gifts to those who need them, they will break out in thanksgiving to God. So two good things will happen: the needs of people will be met and they will joyfully express their thanksgiving to God. You will be glorifying God through your generous gifts. For your generosity to them will prove that you are obedient to the Good News of Christ. (2 Corinthians 9:10-13)

Suppose you see a brother or sister who has no food or clothing, and you say, "Good-bye and have a good day; stay warm and eat well"—but then you don't give that person any food or clothing. What good does that do? So you see, faith by itself isn't enough. Unless it produces good deeds, it is dead and useless. (James 2:15-17)

We know what real love is because Jesus gave up his life for us. So we also ought to give up our lives for our brothers and sisters. If someone has enough money to live well and sees a brother or sister in need but shows no compassion— how can God's love be in that person? Dear children, let's not merely say that we love each other; let us show the truth by our actions. (1 John 3:16-18)

Yet true godliness with contentment is itself great wealth. After all, we brought nothing with us when we came into the world, and we can't take anything with us when we leave it. So if we have enough food and clothing, let us be content. But people who long to be rich fall into temptation and are trapped by many foolish and harmful desires that plunge them into ruin and destruction. For the love of money is the root of all kinds of evil. And some people, craving money, have wandered from the true faith and pierced themselves with many sorrows. (1 Timothy 6:6-10)

Teach those who are rich in this world not to be proud and not to trust in their money, which is so unreliable. Their trust should be in God, who richly gives us all we need for our enjoyment. Tell them to use their money to do good. They should be rich in good works and generous to those in need, always being ready to share with others. By doing this they will be storing up their treasure as a good foundation for the future so that they may experience true life. (1 Timothy 6:17-19)

Why I Visit My Sponsored Kids and Sponsor with Compassion

The Number One reason why I choose to visit my sponsored kids is because I see myself doing nothing less than following God's own example. As lofty as that sounds, let me explain.

Before Jesus came to earth, people knew that God loved them but the relationship was a lot more distant, maintained by priests and sacrifices. When Jesus came to earth from heaven as a man, this added a whole new level to our relationship. Now we can be absolutely sure that God loves us because He proved it by coming from heaven to be with us and dying for our sins. No more can we shake our fists at the angry deity in the sky saying, *"You don't understand what I'm going through!"* In His life on earth Jesus experienced everything we do, the good and the bad: grief, sorrow, rejection, loneliness, anger, pain, hunger, tiredness. Through Jesus we are connected to God, the Creator of the universe.

In the same way, our sponsored children know we love them through our gifts, money, letters and photos. However, there is always distance between us. When you make the decision to sacrifice whatever you need to in order to go and be with them, to enter their lives in person, this adds a whole other dimension to your relationship. By being with someone you are truly showing how much you care, above and beyond thoughts, prayers and any other assistance.

It is worth any sacrifice you need to make.

Why I Sponsor with Compassion
As a Christian I believe I am responsible for using what God has given me to help bring others into His Kingdom. I would put my involvement with Compassion down to one word: HOPE. I am by no means an expert on poverty but from what I've seen and experienced in 12 countries, the most devastating aspect of poverty is the lack of hope. People look at the situations and circumstances they're in, their past and their future,

and see no way out. No way that it can be any different for them or their children.

Compassion changes all this. Yes, they provide assistance with food, medical care, education and income-generating skills, but none of these provide true hope for the future. As a Christian, I am convinced that true hope for this life and the next comes from a relationship with Jesus. No one in the Compassion programs is forced to believe anything, but when a person is consistently face-to-face with the overwhelming, relentless, extravagant love of Jesus, given freely with no strings attached, it must be hard to resist.

Since embracing the reality that all I have belongs to God and I am just looking after it for Him, I have chosen to live simply and am content with a roof over my head, food on the table and clothes on my back. This has enabled me to give a substantial part of my income as a teacher toward child sponsorship and visiting the kids I sponsor.

Reflecting on my experiences in the developing world, I love seeing the number of situations where I had nothing to offer but *prayer*. I didn't necessarily like being in those situations at the time because I felt so useless, helpless and inadequate but as God says to Paul in 2 Corinthians *"My strength is made perfect in weakness."* That statement rang true on too many occasions.

Being able to pray with and for these precious families was such a humbling experience and a privilege, I often struggled to hold it together. The fact we can come directly to the Creator of the Universe and He listens and responds to us. He *wants* to hear from us and *yearns* to have a relationship with us.

I was able to pray for a miracle of healing. For provision of jobs, houses and food. For strength, courage, wisdom and knowledge. For God's peace and security to come on each family. For barriers to be broken down so that the families would fully come to know and rely on God for their needs. I was also able to pray for a beautiful group of 13-15 year old girls on behalf of their sponsors who most likely will never get to visit them.

I was left with the profound realization that when everything else is stripped away and we're left with nothing but complete and utter dependence on God, that's when He does His best and most powerful work.

I have been on the Compassion journey and have just spent the year living off my savings in the Philippines because I am following God, doing what I believe He wants me to do. That's my motivation, pure and simple. People in the developed world, including many Christians, chase after things like security, safety, comfort and ease. However, my understanding of the Bible tells me following God and even life in general is not always going to be safe, secure, comfortable or easy. It sure hasn't been for me. It's often risky and dangerous, both in a physical and emotional sense, but it comes down to *"If we go on this journey of following God, do we trust Him to keep the promises He has given us in His word?"* Do we trust Him?

If you haven't already, I encourage you to join me and many others in this journey of following God. Be a part of His eternal epic rather than insisting on being the boss of your own life. Seriously, it's like the choice between having a supporting role in a long-running majestic Broadway musical or being the star of a twenty-minute kindergarten play. Find out what He's wired you up to do and do it to serve and help others. Use your gifts and talents (everybody has them!) for God's glory rather than your own. For eternity. I guarantee you won't regret it.

Looking back, I can see how God has used these last seven years of Compassion sponsorship to change my life and develop my character in so many ways: heart for the poor, contentment, living simply and giving generously, investing my time, money, emotions and resources in something greater than myself–His eternal Kingdom.

A Final Challenge

I really hope you have been inspired, encouraged and challenged by my story, which is really one small chapter in God's eternal epic tale.

Can I encourage you to join me and become a Compassion sponsor? I hope that through this book you have felt a sense of the genuine impact that child sponsorship with Compassion has on individuals, families and communities.

One day we will all be accountable to God for the way we have used what He has given us. He has also given us free will. This is a double-edged sword: we have a choice to make, and with that choice comes consequences that affect ourselves and others. You can choose to use what you have been given to fund a lifestyle of comfort, convenience, security and ease for yourself. Or you can choose to make your life count on earth and in eternity by using your time, money and resources to help and invest in other people. Encouraging, loving and providing for them.

There are many ways to do this, but I believe without doubt Compassion is one of the most effective and I hope that I have shown that one person can change the life of one child (or more) if they choose to. The integrity is through-the-roof and lives are being transformed. Around the world, former sponsored children are becoming doctors, nurses, dentists, journalists, teachers, Pastors, engineers, even senators and government leaders!

I'm going to give the final words to a Compassion graduate (one of the many success stories) from Colombia. At a meeting in 2012 he was asked to explain why people should sponsor with Compassion, and speaking from his personal experience this is what he said:

> "It's not about food. It's not about money. It's not even about love, but it's about changing a life.

At the end of the day it's not what Compassion does, but it's what God does through Compassion."

Compassion International is God's business and it WORKS.

Websites

Compassion International
www.compassion.com
www.compassion.com.au (Compassion Australia)

David Chalmers (trip photos and videos)
Blog: supernintendo81.blogspot.com
YouTube: www.youtube.com/user/dccompassion

Pastor's Discipleship Network (Richmond Wandera)
www.pdnafrica.org

Made In Hope (Michelle Tolentino)
www.madeinhope.org

Just a Minute (Dr Wess Stafford)
www.justaminute.com

The Man With 50 Kids (by Chad Loftis)
http://vimeo.com/71016925

Mercy House of the Philippines (Nikki and Anthony Esquivel)
bringinghomezeke.blogspot.com
www.facebook.com/mercyphilippines
www.americanhelper.org/?post_causes=mercy-house

Hope Created Philippines (Dan and Marlene Bray)
hopecreated.com
www.facebook.com/pages/Hope-Created/176708612372935
bewarethecomfortzone.com

Ruel Foundation
Website: www.ruelfoundation.com
Blog: ruelfoundation.blogspot.com
YouTube: www.youtube.com/user/ruelfoundation2014

About the Author

David Chalmers was born in 1981 in the city of Melbourne in Victoria, Australia, and is the eldest son of a Pastor and a teacher. He is a Primary school teacher and has taught at several schools around Victoria, sharing his passion for music and sport.

David has also spent time as a musician, statistician, website administrator, amateur sports journalist and basketball coach, and is a doting uncle to three nephews and two nieces.

Having grown up in a Christian home, David committed his life to Jesus in 2001 at age 20 and hasn't looked back. He has served in several churches, leading worship, communion, preaching, kid's ministry and playing bass guitar and drums.

David started sponsoring with Compassion International in 2006, and over the last seven years God captured his heart so fully with His love for the poor, he financially sponsored 54 children and visited 31 of them in 12 countries.

In 2014 David volunteered at an orphanage in the Philippines called *The Ruel Foundation*. He taught the children English and introduced hundreds of new people to the work of Ruel through the Facebook page and blog.

He blogs at http://supernintendo81.blogspot.com

Made in United States
Orlando, FL
01 July 2022